GOLF'S MENTAL MAGIC

Grateful thanks go to . . .

Golf Gifts of Lombard, Illinois, for their permission to use the quotes at the opening of each chapter.

Getting The Edge Company, of Cleveland, Ohio, for their permission to use the Jack Nicklaus quote in Chapter Four and the Hale Irwin quote in Chapter Twelve. These quotes are reprinted from The Edge, by Howard E. Ferguson. Copyright 1990, 800 Playhouse Square Plaza, 1220 Huron Road, Cleveland, OH, 44115.

GOLF'S MENTAL MAGIC

Dr. GUY S. FASCIANA
FOREWORD BY HALE IRWIN

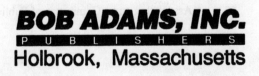

BOB ADAMS, INC.
PUBLISHERS
Holbrook, Massachusetts

Published by Bob Adams, Inc.
260 Center Street, Holbrook, MA 02343

ISBN: 1-55850-066-9

Printed in the United States of America

A B C D E F G H I J

FOREWORD

It has been said and agreed upon by many professionals and amateurs that golf is 80 percent mental and 20 percent physical. While those percentages may be loosely applied to each individual, it is my feeling that the mental aspects of the game are fundamentally more important than the physical.

In my years of playing golf it has been my continuing effort to establish a sound mental approach to the basic swing elements and management of my golf game. Hitting hundreds of golf balls can do you little good if you do not use your brain while practicing. I would suggest quality practice rather than quantity to achieve your goal.

With these comments of mine you may well find this book to further enhance these principles upon which my game is predicated.

— *Hale Irwin*

ACKNOWLEDGMENTS

Many touring golf professionals were gracious in granting interviews during my research for *Golf's Mental Magic*. I wish to thank PGA Tour players Bruce Devlin, Bill Buttner, Emlyn Aubrey, Billy Mayfair, Dave Ogrin, John Cook, Tom Ubank, and Sonny Skinner. I also wish to thank LPGA players Peggy Kirsch, Amy Benz, Barbara Mucha, Kathy Whitworth, Nancy Lopez, and Collene Walker.

Special thanks to Hale Irwin for writing a very complimentary forward. I also want to thank Thomas Galvin, Director of Junior Golf, PGA of America for his comments. Thanks to Art Wall, Jonathan Rinkevich, and Jeff Reich for their remarks.

Last and most important, I want to thank my wife Jane for her support, encouragement, and feedback and for making golf fun for me. Jane did a great job on the illustrations!

THE AUTHOR

Guy S. Fasciana earned a Doctor of Dental Medicine degree from the University of Pittsburgh School of Dental Medicine, Pittsburgh, Pennsylvania, and masters degrees in Health Education and Sport Psychology from the University of Arizona, Tucson, Arizona. Dr. Fasciana has taught courses in Stress Management and Peak Performance at the University of Arizona and Introduction to Health Care at Pima Community College. He currently facilitates clinics and workshops in golf, stress management, and personal development. Dr. Fasciana counsels amateur sports enthusiasts as well as professional golfers.

Dr. Fasciana wrote *Are Your Dental Fillings Poisoning You?* (Keat's Publishing, 1986), an evaluation of the dental controversy about the health implications of mercury dental fillings. He has had various dental articles appear in the national magazines, *Bestways, 20th Century Living*, and *The Human Ecologist*.

In October, 1988, *Fitness Magazine* published "Overdoing Exercise Can Make You Sick." This article alerted fitness trainers of the risk of illnesses like colds and flu resulting from overexercising and provided guidelines to develop and monitor healthful exercise programs.

Dr. Fasciana has written other papers about personal development, stress management, and sports enhancement. Some of the topics include the relationship between stress and performance, the relationship between stress and health, the relationship between subliminal messages and performance, self-esteem and sport performance, assertiveness, and the effects of exercise on the immune system.

In *Golf's Mental Magic*, Dr. Fasciana draws from his knowledge and experience to teach you how to achieve mental, physical, and emotional fitness; how to manage stress, how to manage your thoughts; how to improve your golf game; and how to have fun—especially how to have fun! He writes in a style that nurtures your love and understanding of the game.

CONTENTS

SECTION C:
STEPPING UP FROM BASICS:
IMPROVING YOUR GOLF FUNDAMENTALS

SECTION D:
FUELING FOR THE WHOLE NINE YARDS: GETTING IN SHAPE

SECTION E:
GOLF PSYCHOLOGY: MAKING YOUR MIND YOUR ALLY

CHAPTER 12
STRESS MANAGEMENT:
GETTING OUT OF YOUR OWN WAY
Mental Skills—Managing Your Emotions

SECTION F:
APPENDICES

INTRODUCTION

Winner	*Loser*
Always part of the answer	Always part of the problem
Always has a plan	Always has an excuse
Says "Let me do it for you."	Says "That's not my job."
Sees an answer for every problem	Sees a problem for every solution
Sees the green near the sand trap	Sees the sand trap near the green
Says "It may be difficult but	Says "It may be possible but
it is possible."	it's too difficult."

Which would you like to be?

Have you ever found yourself playing golf with someone who struck the golf ball really well? He didn't look as if he would play well, but he did. He didn't look strong or coordinated, but he hit the ball a mile. In the deep recesses of your mind, you probably asked yourself: "What is his secret? What does he know that I don't know?"

What does it take to play well? Does it take proper equipment, a good teacher, a positive mental approach, or natural talent? These are all important. Playing with equipment you are suited to will help you to reach your golf potential, although I've seen golfers shoot scores in the mid-seventies with rented clubs. A good golf instructor can help you to select the proper equipment and teach you the fundamentals of the game and how to manage the golf course, if you are willing to take a few lessons. A good sports psychologist can teach you a positive approach to learning the fundamentals and applying them on the course, and can teach you how to manage yourself on the course so that you don't get in your own way. Of course, this requires some lessons as well, or a good book on golf psychology.

What about natural talent? Natural talent is about as important as acquired talent. You see, practically everyone can learn how to play golf. I may not be able to put you on tour, but I can teach you how to have fun and enjoy the game of golf.

Perhaps the most important ability for you to acquire is that of assessment, knowing when the problem you are having on the golf course is related to equipment, mechanical skills, or mental skills. I wish I had a dollar for every time I heard conversations like the ones that follow. The scene is a golf shop. A man of about fifty is talking with a salesperson about the new putter he has in his hands. "Until a few years ago, I could putt with the best of them. Lately, I can't seem to get the ball in the hole. I guess it's time for a new putter."

A woman in her thirties is talking with another salesperson. "Which are the clubs that are supposed to help you to get the ball in the air? I can't seem to get my golf ball off the ground."

And a young man says, "I want a new set of clubs that will help me to hit the ball straighter. You know, some of those forgiving clubs. The ball seems to start off in the direction where I want it to go and then takes a right turn."

Golfers are a rare breed. We prefer to buy a new putter, new clubs, or a different brand of golf ball than try to learn why we are missing putts, hitting grounders, or slicing the ball. Not that we don't worry about technique. We golfers will extract tips from golf magazines, fellow players, or even strangers on the practice range. Anything to help us to hit the ball further and straighter. We will talk relentlessly about what we did correctly during the last "shot" that made it go the way it did, or what we did incorrectly that caused the ball to skirt off the way it did. During dinner we will re-hash every shot of every hole, to the dismay of others at the dinner table. When we come up with an idea we think will help our golf game, we will rush to the practice range or golf course to try it out.

Is this behavior unusual? Not really. People are accustomed to learning through trial and error. We try to perform a task, and when we don't succeed, we try it again. If the second attempt is not successful, we change the way we did it and try again.

I learned to play golf by the trial-and-error method. I first picked up a golf club when I was a freshman in college—a pretty old dude when you consider that most of today's touring pro's learned to golf when they were seven or eight years old. One of my friends asked me to go with him to the "driving" range to hit some balls. When we got there, we picked a couple of clubs and went out to the hitting area. The club I picked was a driver; back then a driver was the only choice you had if you didn't have your own golf clubs. So I asked my buddy, "OK, how do I hit the ball?" "Just stand like this and swing at the ball as hard as you can and see how far you can hit it," he replied. Because I knew that his father played golf, I figured that my friend knew what he was talking about. So that was our goal: to see how far we could hit the ball. I hate to admit this, but I didn't hit the ball very far.

After a couple of visits to the driving range, we decided to go to a golf course and play. I borrowed some clubs and went golfing. Back then, it seemed everyone was an expert. It didn't matter that no one knew how to play; everyone thought they had figured out how to hit that little white ball "really far." So it went, the blind leading the blind. We kept learning from each other and practicing what we learned until we really got good at repeating the wrong way to swing a golf club.

"Trial and error" learning is not the most efficient way to learn. Correct learning can take place three ways: by auditory (hearing), by seeing (visual), or by feeling (kinesthetic). These methods are discribed in educational learning theory. I prefer to modify this theory and identify three methods that I find helpful in understanding how we learn. These methods are: intellectual, visual, and kinesthetic.

Learning through *understanding* appeals to the intellectuals, people who want information about what they are about to learn. This knowledge gives them an understanding of how to perform the activity and reduces any anxiety or tension created by the lack of knowledge or fear of failure. You can gather information about how to golf by reading books, by talking with someone (preferably a golf pro), by watching video tapes, or by listening to audio tapes.

A method that appeals to many people is that of *imitation* (visual method). In other words, you observe models and imitate their behavior. A model could be your favorite sports figure, such as Greg Norman or Nancy Lopez, or it could be a teacher or parent. This system of learning is relatively successful. How many kids, when asked, "Who is your favorite football player?" would respond "Joe Montana" with a throwing gesture mimicking their favorite quarterback?

With the third method of learning, *kinesthetic learning*, someone actually moves your arms, hands, or legs in the correct positions. You program your mind to remember the feelings and positions. This programming is called "muscle memory" and is a very effective learning method.

Which method is most appropriate for you? It depends on how you learn. When you learned how to dance, did you learn by watching the other kids dance, did you learn by someone explaining the steps, or did you learn by someone moving you into position? To discover how you learn skills, listen to the language you use when someone is explaining something to you. Do you respond with "Yes, I see," "I hear you," "Yes, I understand," or "Show me how?"

❑ If you respond with "Yes, I see," you may be a *visual person* and may learn best by watching someone demonstrate a skill. In this case, you may benefit from instructional videotapes that have a model demonstrate the correct movement over and over.

❑ If you respond with "Yes, I hear you," you may be an auditory learner. In this case, your understanding may be improved by verbal instruction, someone explaining how to do something verbally or in writing.

❑ A response of "Yes, I understand," suggests that you learn through the assimilation of information and that knowledge is essential for your successful performance. You probably learn well by asking questions and getting information.

❑ A response such as "Show me how" indicates that you learn by having someone demonstrate and help you to move your body into position.

One of these methods will probably suit you better than the others, but I suggest you learn the motor skills of the golf swing, chipping, pitching, and putting in two or three different methods, if possible. Each method reinforces the other methods. When you combine information, imitation, and kinesthetics, your success rate increases dramatically. What method do I use in *Golf's Mental Magic*? All three. The information, drills, and exercises will help you to learn through all three channels.

And if information, kinesthetic instruction, and modeling can increase your success rate, just think what practice can do for you. Practice reinforces the skills you have observed and provides feedback for those you were taught. Use as many of your senses as possible and you can improve your success rate. If you are told (verbal) how to perform, watch (visual) a demonstration, and have a golf professional move (kinesthetic) your body into the correct position, your chances of success are increased through practice.

ORGANIZATION OF *GOLF'S MENTAL MAGIC*

Quite a few years ago, while I was still in the struggling stage of my golf game, I would sometimes begin to play a really good round of golf. During my round I would think to myself, "Now I've got it. I've figured out what this game is all about. I know how to hit the ball well." A few holes later, I would hit a poor tee shot and get into trouble. I would attempt some miracle recovery shot. This usually didn't work, and I would put myself into greater difficulty. Then I would push harder and swing harder. I would begin hitting some poor shots, and before I knew it, I was thinking to myself, "I'm never going to learn how to play this game." I made *all* the mistakes I could: I never learned good golf fundamentals, I didn't know course strategy, I would lose confidence as soon as I hit a poor shot, I would lose concentration with the slightest amount of pressure, and I would get stressed out. Once in a while everything would come together and I would play well, only to find that the "magic" was gone as soon as I got into the slightest trouble. I couldn't forget the poor shot I made six holes back. When I lost the "feel," I didn't know how to get it back. My concentration would come and go. I didn't know how to visualize my golf shot. Looking back, I am amazed that I continued to play despite the frustration that I experienced.

Today, things are different. After a few golf lessons and graduate degrees in sports psychology and stress management, I play a pretty respectable game of golf. Sure, I still hit a poor shot or two or have an occasional poor round, but I have a solid foundation of sound golf fundamentals. I learned how to play smart, how to get out of trouble using the percentage shots, how to get back the "feel" when it goes away, how to manage stress, and how to visualize my golf performance before I execute my shot. I have also learned how to block out poor shots. I block out these shots so effectively that my wife thinks I cheat, since I have no recall of one or two shots per round!

I have learned a lot over the years and have taught my students well. The success of my students has inspired me to write this book. If you follow my instructions, you can't help improving your golf game.

The philosophy behind *Golf's Mental Magic* is this: *preparation leads to success*! The ability to improve your performance in golf depends on preparation. You need to prepare *physically*, *mentally*, and *emotionally*.

❏ You need to prepare *physically* by learning the fundamentals of golf and elevating your physical fitness through sound nutrition and exercise.

❏ You need to prepare mentally by learning how to believe in yourself, how to have a positive mental approach, how to maintain the appropriate level of sports arousal through relaxation exercises and thought control, how to set attainable goals, how to visualize your golf shots, and how to preview your performance.

❏ You need to prepare emotionally by learning how to identify and remove barriers that prevent you from reaching your goals, and you need to learn how to get out of your own way.

Golf's Mental Magic contains four distinct strategies. These strategies are integrated to give one continuous flow of information. The first strategy, Managing Your Mind, begins in the first chapter and continues throughout the book. The second strategy, Sports Nutrition (Chapter 9) and Sports Fitness (Chapter 10), is designed to improve physical fitness and enhance energy, concentration, and endurance. The third strategy, Learning the Mental Skills, an integral part of each chapter, is designed to help you to learn and apply golf fundamentals. The fourth strategy, Peak Performance (Chapter 11), and Stress Management (Chapter 12), is designed to teach you mental skills to control stress, emotions, and excitement on the golf course so your natural talent can reveal itself. I have placed the chapters on Peak Performance and Stress Management at the end not because they are less important but because they are more meaningful once you have used the mental approach to learn and apply the fundamentals. They are the icing on the cake!

Each chapter is further organized into three sections: *golf fundamentals* and the mental approach to these fundamentals, *learning the mental skills* or psychological principles to enhance performance, and *integration exercises*, which teach you how to integrate your mind and body. The knowledge you gain from reading my book will help you to improve your golf game, to increase your enjoyment of the game, and to elevate your satisfaction of the "game of a lifetime."

If you look at the table of contents, you will see a progression of chapters. The chapters are arranged to allow you to learn the simple tasks before you learn the more complex ones. Chapter 1 teaches you how to get ready to play golf. Chapter 2 teaches you how to play smart golf. Just by reading these two chapters you will learn enough to lower your golf score immediately. If you spend a few minutes thinking ahead each time you play your home course, you will find that you can play each hole in a variety of ways and you will be able to select a plan that matches your game. For example, take a short, par 4,310-yard hole. You could use your driver and a pitching wedge, or you could use a 3 wood and an 8 iron or you could use two 5 irons. Once you decide on a strategy, use the advantages available to achieve the best performance.

The chapters in the second section teach you how to approach the most elementary golf skills such as grip, alignment, stance, and timing. By developing a consistent routine for approaching the golf ball, you will build a consistent swing that will, in turn, help you to play consistent golf.

The chapters in the third section teach you the mental approach to golf fundamentals. Four chapters cover putting, chipping, pitching, and the full shots. The chapter on putting comes first. Why putting first? Because it is easier to learn simple skills first. These simple skills pave the way for you to learn the more complex skills used in the full swing.

The chapters in the fourth section will help you to become nutritionally and physically fit. This is important because nutrition, exercise, and agility are *directly* related to your alertness, energy, stamina, concentration, and confidence.

In the last section, chapter 11 will teach you how to develop the characteristics of a winner, and chapter 12 will teach you how to manage stress on the golf course. The lessons learned in these two chapters will carry over to other parts of your life, and you will soon find that you are happier about yourself—an unexpected bonus!

Mental skills segment
Each chapter has a mental skills section called SKULL PRACTICE: LEARNING THE MENTAL SKILLS. The mental skills sections make up a sub-program that will teach you how to believe in yourself, how to manage time, how to relax, and how to handle stress. The exercises in the chapters will help you to control your thoughts and stay positive, to visualize your golf performance, and to learn how to

get out of your own way. *I strongly urge you to perform the exercises as you read each chapter*. This is not a "quick-fix" book. The structure is designed to allow you to learn all the elements of peak performance. Take your time and you will benefit enormously from reading my book. Another reward for sticking to my plan is that you will learn patience, a valuable tool in all walks of life.

Integrated golf

This book is meant to supplement instruction by a PGA teaching professional or information received from books on golf fundamentals. It is not designed to replace professional instruction. I discuss mechanics, in general terms, so that you can understand the mental components of those mechanics. The information that I provide connects your mind and your body so you can begin to play what I like to call *integrated* golf. The books I have read about golf discuss either golf fundamentals or the mental aspects of the golf. *Golf's Mental Magic* is the only book that integrates both mechanics and mental skills in such a way that you can learn to play better golf.

WHAT TO EXPECT FROM THIS BOOK

> "In every tournament there are a few rounds of super golf; without a doubt they are played subconsciously."
>
> — *Chick Evens, Jr.*
> Golf Professional

You can reasonably expect to learn to play better golf and to reduce your handicap by one or two strokes almost immediately upon reading and applying the information in chapters 1 and 2. As you read chapters 3 and 4, you will experience a slight temporary decline in performance because you are now paying attention to the mental aspects of the game. Once you learn and practice the mental aspects, they will become part of your routine. When they become part of your routine, you will stop thinking about them consciously and you will begin to make dramatic improvement. *This is a temporary inconvenience for a permanent improvement.*

In reading chapters 5 through 8, you will notice an improvement in your approach to the different golf strokes and experience a noticeable improvement again. Chapters 9 and 10 will have a general effect on your golf game and, depending on your current diet and current exercise program, may have some immediate improvement.

The effect of chapters 11 and 12 will be similar to the effect of chapters 2 and 3. There may be a temporary decline in performance followed by a rapid improvement.

You can minimize the temporary decline in performance by practicing the exercises and drills according to my schedule and to practice them on the practice range and not the course.

— *Guy Fasciana*
San Antonio, Texas

SECTION A:

STRATEGIC PLANNING: KNOW
WHERE YOU WANT TO GO

"Set goals for yourself and work your hardest to
achieve them. Some goals you will achieve and
others you won't, but at least you will have the satisfaction of knowing where you were going."

— *Beth Daniel*
Professional Golfer

Have you heard about the guy who trained a gorilla to hit golf balls? Every day he took the gorilla, Godzilla, to the practice range. Godzilla would go up to the golf ball and hit it 350 yards every time. One day the trainer decided to take Godzilla to the golf course. Everyone gathered around the first tee to see what was going on. Godzilla set up to the golf ball and swung the golf club. To the amazement of everyone watching, Godzilla hit the golf ball 350 yards. With the ball lying about 75 yards from the green, Godzilla hit his second shot. The golf ball went over the green . . . about 275 yards over the green.

The moral of this story is that golf is a mental game. Sure, you can learn to cream the golf ball, but to score well, you must learn to use your head as well as your muscles. We will begin our journey toward playing better golf by discussing a couple of strategies that will quickly shave strokes from your game. By reading chapters 1 and 2, you will begin to play smarter golf. Playing smarter golf will help you to play better golf. Playing better golf will lower your scores. It is as simple as that. This is sort of an instant fix for your game—something that we all appreciate from time to time. However, it is not a "band-aid" fix. These strategies are based on research in sports psychology and built on sound principles that work. These principles can help the weekend athlete as well as the Olympic champion.

Chapter 1 will teach you how to prepare to play golf: what to do on the day before the match, what to do on the day of the match, and how to warm up before the match. Chapter 2 will teach you how to prepare to play the course and how to plan your strategy for playing each hole. As you read through the subsequent sections of this book, you will learn how to improve your level of play by using the mental skills I will teach you. In this way you will be better able to lower your score even more.

CHAPTER 1:

PRE-ROUND STRATEGY: GETTING

READY TO PLAY GOLF

"It's hard to separate the mental and the physical. So
much of what you do physically happens because
you've thought about it and mentally prepared for it."
— *Dan Fouts*
Professional Football Player

Several years ago, when I practiced dentistry in Pennsylvania, I often played golf
on Wednesday afternoons with three other dentists. Two of these gentlemen had a
rivalry going. Allow me to tell you about it.

First a little background. Dentist A and dentist B had office hours on Wednesday mornings. Each finished at the office in plenty of time to get to the country club
for a one o'clock tee time. Dentist A was my partner. Dentist B was the partner of
dentist D. Dentist A, who usually drove by a fast food restaurant on the way to the
club, would set the tee time for 1:00 pm. He would then tell B that the tee time was
at 12:45 pm. Dentist B was irritated thinking he wouldn't have enough time to get
to the club and eat his sandwich in the restaurant before starting our round of golf.

This is the scenario that occurred almost weekly. B would zip into the parking
lot, run into the building, order a hamburger and fries, rush to change into his golf
clothes, dash to the pro shop, sign for the cart, pick up his hamburger and fries, and
race to the first tee where everyone was waiting for him. For the first few holes, the
dialogue went like this:

B to A: "Why do you always make the tee time so early?"
A: "Why can't you be more efficient at the office?"

B: "I am efficient."
A: "It's a miracle to get you here on time."

This went on for a few holes. Back and forth. In addition to the dialogue, B was miss-hitting shots, missing shots to the green, and missing two-to-three foot putts for the first few holes. When B missed his two-to-three foot putts, A would remark softly, but loudly enough for B to hear, "Watch this . . . and he's taking lessons to play like that!" Our team usually won the match.

Needless to say, these circumstances were not conducive for dentist B to play his best. Many golfers let their situations upset them and disrupt their pace. In this chapter I will teach you how to prepare for a match (round of golf or a tournament) so that you will have the best chance to play well no matter what the situation.

STRATEGY FOR THE DAY BEFORE THE MATCH

General activities.
What you do on the day *before* playing golf can affect the way you play. Even what you eat is important. I had a racquetball client who liked Mexican food but often got heartburn after eating it. On the night before an important tournament, he ate at a Mexican restaurant. He didn't sleep very well and, as a result, played poorly the next day against players over whom he had almost always prevailed. Caffeine can also cause a decline in performance. If you drink coffee before going to bed, it may interfere with your sleep. There are other examples of how diet affects performance in chapter 9.

Activities that make you over-tired may reduce your restful sleep, resulting in a tired feeling on the day of the match. Avoid going shopping after dinner if you need to unwind before retiring.

Tasks that exhaust your muscles will have a tendency to reduce your "feel" for the golf shot. For example, you would not want to chop a cord of firewood or plant a vegetable garden the night before a tournament. Either of these activities may strain the muscles of your arms and legs reducing your effectiveness on the golf course.

Daily routines.
We are all at our most comfortable when we have a regular routine. Most people go to bed at about the same time, wake up at about the same time, eat at the same time, and so forth. If you deviate greatly from your routine, you will feel out of sync. When you are out of sync, you feel uncomfortable. If you are accustomed to eating dinner at 6:00 pm and you must wait until 8:00 pm, this change in your routine will probably be uncomfortable or irritable. If you sleep longer than usual in the morn-

ing, your rhythm will be off track. If you stay up well beyond your bedtime, you will not react as usual the next day.

Each of us tends to do certain tasks in a specific order. If, at dinner, you are accustomed to eating your meat first and potato last, you will tend to want to keep eating that way. Each of us tends to put on one shoe before the other each time we get dressed.

The more aware you are of your routine, the more you can maintain it. The more you maintain your routine, the better you will play. What I'm telling you is that you should *become aware of your routine and stick to it.* Let's say you are in a club championship tournament and your tee time is at 11:00 am. During your normal work week, you get up at 6:30 am, have breakfast, take a shower, and go to work at 8:00 am. The night before the tournament you decide that three hours is too much time to spend between getting ready to leave the house and playing, so you go to bed an hour later and get up an hour later in order to have only two hours between getting ready to leave the house and playing in the tournament. Good strategy? I think not. By delaying your routine an hour, you'll upset your biorhythm, meaning you won't feel the way you normally do. You also won't play golf the way you normally do.

This strategy is not conducive to the best performance. How would you change it for your benefit? I think a better strategy might be to retire at your usual time, awake at your usual time, and read a relaxing book or article for an hour, say, 8:00 am to 9:00 am. Your choice of reading material is important. Ideally, you would read something mentally and physically relaxing. You would not want to read a book on golf mechanics or mental preparation for peak performance on the morning of the tournament. You would also want to avoid doing something strenuous, like cutting the grass, which can tire your muscles and reduce your feel for a good golf swing.

Relaxation exercises.
The relationship between sports arousal and peak performance is discussed in chapter 11. If you develop a routine for conducting relaxation exercises, you can use this routine the night before a match or during the hour before you play. Relaxation techniques are useful for general body relaxation, for mental relaxation, and in creating visualization routines. Visualization can significantly improve your golf game. So that morning, you could do a relaxation exercise and visualize yourself playing excellent golf. As you read through this book, I will teach you how to use some effective relaxation techniques.

What to do the day before the match

❏ Eat your normal diet in the usual proportions, avoiding problem foods.

❏ Do your regular exercise routine, whether it is jogging, walking, or whatever. Avoid weight training; it could stress your muscles.

❑ Participate in low-stress activities, avoiding activities that could tire your muscles.

❑ Take it easy and relax.

❑ Go to bed at your regular time.

❑ Avoid taking any non-prescription medications that you do not routinely take. Medications such as antihistamines can take the edge off your concentration.

❑ Plan what you are going to do from the moment you get up to the moment you tee off. Write your plan in your diary.

❑ Make peace with everyone who is important to you.

STRATEGY FOR THE DAY OF THE MATCH

General activities.
On the day of the match you want to have a "business-as-usual" attitude. Get up at your regular time, eat your regular breakfast, and follow your plan for what you are going to do from the time you get up to the time you tee off.

Relaxed pace.
You want to maintain a relaxed pace. The pace at which you begin your day is the pace at which you will play golf. If that is not your optimal pace, you need to adjust it. You may want to consider using relaxation exercises (described at the end of each chapter).

What to avoid on the day of the match.
Hassles, arguments, tax returns, and other sources of stress.
    The following guidelines may put you on the right track. On the day of the match do the following:

❑ Wake up to relaxing music. Do not wake up to an alarm or heavy rock music. (If you are not convinced that this is a good idea, set your alarm to "alarm" instead of music on a day when you are not going to play.) Pay attention to your heart rate when the buzzer goes off. Is it relaxed or beating a hundred miles an hour? When you wake up with your heart racing, you will understand what I am trying to say.

❑ Do one task at a time. If you are one of these people who enjoys doing two or three tasks at once, you may want to reassess this strategy, not only for the day of the match but for your life in general.

❑ Do everything slowly. Set the pace for your golf game.

❑ Resolve anything that may divert your attention from play. Be sure you can resolve anything you start. If you cannot finish or resolve something, write the problem on a sheet of paper and list your options for resolving it. This strategy also works if you cannot sleep on the night before a match. If you are lying awake and cannot sleep and something is on your mind, get up and write down whatever it is. You will be surprised how quickly you fall asleep.

❑ Finish any emotional business with your loved ones. If you have had an argument with your husband, wife, children, or other significant person in your life, resolve it before you go to play your match.

❑ Drive slowly. Do not rush to the course. Do this even if you have to fight yourself to contain your adrenalin. See Skull Practice on stress and time management.

Warmup exercises.
When many golfers think of warming up, they think of hitting a bucket of balls with their driver. A serious golfer will broaden his or her idea of warmup exercises to include stretching. Such people have a set warmup routine. When I was at the Tournament Players Club for the Northern Telecom Tucson Open in January, 1990, one of the younger players, Emlyn Aubrey, impressed me with his warmup routine. Aubrey arrived on the practice range and slowly began stretching exercises, first for the lower body, then for the upper body. After stretching, he began some timing and rhythm exercises. The he checked his fundamentals (alignment, posture, grip). Soon he began pitching some shots to about fifty yards. He worked his way up to full-pitch shots, then proceeded to another short iron, worked his way up to the woods, and then to the driver. Finally, he went to the putting green to practice.

Aubrey's warmup process took him about fifteen minutes for the stretching and timing exercises, about thirty minutes swinging through the various clubs, and about fifteen minutes for putting. Perhaps you don't have this much time or are unwilling to spend an hour warming up. Whatever your commitment to playing better golf, you can develop a warmup routine and find time to follow it each time you play. I strongly suggest you write out your routine so that you have it on paper. You can alter it as you progress through your golf improvement program. Write down your new routine and keep the written copy of your old routine. It helps to date each sheet of paper and to indicate your level of play at that time.

This is the second time I have suggested writing things down. In all my classes on peak performance, stress management, and personal development, I require the participants to make written records. I believe this is an effective way to become aware of your habitual behavior, to plan which habits you want to change and how you intend to change those habits. Now here, in my opinion, are the essentials of a good warm up routine:

Stretching. When you take a full swing, you stretch the muscles in your arms, legs, and trunk. Slowly stretching these muscles before you play gives you flexibility without injuring your muscles. If you took a full swing without stretching you might pull a muscle, causing pain and hurting your performance. This step doesn't have to take a lot of time—just enough to loosen up your muscles. When you learn to use the relaxation exercises, you can reduce the time needed to stretch your muscles. You will find more information about stretching in chapter 10, Sports Fitness.

Timing or rhythm practice. You can get a feel for timing or rhythm by swinging a club in an easy manner. During this practice, pay attention to your backswing, change of direction, forward motion, and follow-through. In this routine your attention will be on capturing the "feel" of these movements, not on any change in your fundamentals. Practice your fundamentals during a practice session on a day when you were not going to play golf or during a practice session immediately after you play.

Swinging the golf club. Start by hitting some half-shots (9:00 or 10:00 position) to groove the feel you captured in the timing and rhythm part of the warmup. As you feel more confident and comfortable, increase to three-quarter shots (11:00) and then to full shots. You can devote as much or as little time to this as you want, but spend enough time to accomplish your goal.

Visualizing your shot. Visualizing the shot you expect to execute will help you to program your swing. More importantly, it will take your mind off mechanics and on the feel of the swing. Focusing on mechanics during play will cause you to play poorly; focusing on the flight of the ball or the target will help you play better.

Putting practice. In a normal round of golf (eighteen holes, par 72), a scratch golfer is expected to use thirty-six strokes for putting. That is, 50 percent of your golf shots are putting strokes. For this reason, you'll need to include putting programming in your warmup routine. Putting warmup is performed not only to program your stroke and hit some balls in the hole but to enhance your timing and rhythm and help you to establish pace. In addition to these important general aspects of a good golf game, putting improves your confidence and gives you important insight about the speed and break of the greens. If the ground crew has done everything to the practice green—fertilized, top-dressed, aerated, and cut—that they have done to the greens on the course, the speed of the practice green should closely approximate those on the course.

I suggest you decide in what order you want to perform these essentials, write them down, and perform them every time you play golf. Experiment with this order and alter your routine as you see fit. For example, you may want to practice putting first, then go to the practice range. No matter which order you decide on however, stretching is best done at the beginning of your routine.

SKULL PRACTICE: LEARNING THE MENTAL SKILLS

Putting time on your side

Time is important. We need time to work, time to play, and time for important relationships. When we don't have enough time for each of these areas, we feel stressed and anxious. We begin to think perhaps we'll get fired, or we'll alienate our families, or we won't be able to take that needed vacation. This anxiety affects everything we do.

Time management stress comes from one or more of the following:

❏ Preoccupation with tasks that we have to do.

❏ Ineffective pacing—in an attempt to do two tasks at once, we do neither correctly.

❏ Stimulus overload/underload—we become too excited or too bored.

❏ Anxiety—an unidentified feeling that something is wrong.

❏ Negative cycles—

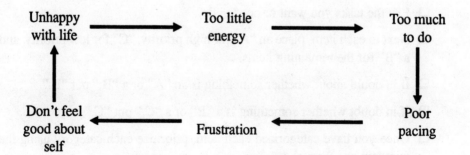

What can you do?

Time management is the process by which you set priorities and schedule tasks in the most efficient order possible. Time management involves your values, goals, and priorities.

There are three major obstacles to effective time management:

Procrastination—putting off an event or activity.

Solution:
❏ Sit down and get started on something.

❏ Give yourself a time slot to devote to a task.

❏ Use your mind to create a way to accomplish your goal.

Perfectionism—wanting everything you do to be perfect.

Solution:
❏ Develop a "hitter's" attitude (Get three out of ten hits)

❏ Focus on long-term goals.

❏ See "unfinished" as an opportunity, not as a problem.

Fear of failure—we see tasks as burdens instead of as challenges.

Solution:
❏ Separate your actions from your self-concept.

❏ Practice positive affirmation statements

❏ Do activities related to the events you fear.

The ABC Method of time management

❏ List the tasks you want or need to do.

❏ Next to each item, place an "A" for high priority, "C" for low priority, and a "B" for the remaining items.

❏ If in doubt about whether something is an "A" or a "B," put "B."

❏ If in doubt whether something is a "B" or a "C," put "C."

❏ Once you have categorized each item, prioritize each category using the numbers one through ten.

In the story that I told you in the beginning of this chapter, dentist B could have solved the problem with work, lunch, and tee times in many ways. He could have decided not to play at all. Or, having decided to play, he could have scheduled fewer patients, made a more appropriate tee time himself, or arranged for lunch by having his assistant call the country club with his order. He could have bought out of the panic that dentist A was trying to dump on him. Then he would have been able to take a relaxed drive to the country club, eat a relaxed lunch, and enjoy a round of golf instead of becoming stressed out. I'll bet you can come up with a few more solutions.

INTEGRATION EXERCISES
Getting your mind and body to work as a unit

Exercises to increase awareness
Awakening log—day before match. On the day before a match, mark down in a log everything that you do from the time you wake up to the time you are ready to leave the house. Note what time you woke up, whether you woke up spontaneously or with the help of the alarm, and everything that you do, in order, from that time. Indicate how you feel during each stage.

      Awakening log—day of match. On the day of the match, repeat the first exercise. After a few days, analyze what you did the day before and the day of the match to see whether you did anything significant.

Exercises to improve time management
      List the tasks you have to do in the next week or so. Apply the ABC Method to this list.

      Take the list and note next to each item whether you are or are not looking forward to that task. If you are not looking forward to doing any task, ask yourself whether this is because of any obstacles to effective time management.

      Ask yourself whether any of the obstacles really apply to you. Can you change your perception of them?

CHAPTER 2:

COURSE STRATEGY: PLAYING

SMART GOLF

"The quality of a person's life is in direct proportion
to their commitment to excellence, regardless of their
chosen field of endeavor."

— *Vince Lombardi*
Football Coach

I often golf at the William Blanchard golf course at Davis-Monthan Air Force Base. William Blanchard is a long, uncomplicated course whose main difficulty is distance, especially from the tee to the bend of the doglegs. The blue tees at William Blanchard are back far enough from the bend in a dogleg that to have an open shot to the green you must hit a long ball. On a typical par 4, dogleg left, you need to drive the golf ball about 240 yards from the blue tees to have a clear shot into the green. From the white tees, you need to hit your tee shot 215 to 220 yards. The average player has less difficulty hitting 215 to 220 yards consistently and so has a more enjoyable time playing from the white tees.

Because William Blanchard golf course is on an air force base, many young airmen play there, some good golfers and some just learning to play. Occasionally I play with a golfer who uses the blue tees when he should really play from the white. Why do I say this? Because these golfers cannot reach the bend in the dogleg with their drive. If a golfer can hit beyond the bend from the blue tees, then the blue tees are appropriate. If not, the white tees are a better choice. If you cannot hit your tee shot to the bend in the dogleg and have a clear shot to the green, you cannot reach the green in regulation. This will cause frustration, and you will think that you are not playing very well even though you may be hitting the golf ball well. Such a situation cannot possibly lead to improved golf and increased satisfaction. Golf played this way just isn't any fun. Read on, because there is a better way.

Why do some players choose the blue tees? Perhaps it is the macho thing so many of us grew up with; perhaps it is a lack of understanding of what the tee boxes represent. If it is a macho thing, many golfers are quickly humbled when they fail to hit the ball past the ladies' tee or hit a slice or a pull-hook out-of-bounds as a result of trying to crunch their drives. Golfers who automatically select the tees furthest back misunderstand the game of golf and mistake it for a contest of distance rather than strategy. *They are thinking checkers instead of chess.*

If a bad choice results from misunderstanding the design of the course, then the golfer needs to learn the purpose of the course design. This is what I want to get across in this chapter. The tee box selection and placement, to stick with our example, are designed to offer a challenge to players of all levels. If you hit a long ball and it lands consistently in the fairway, you will want to tee off from the championship tees. If you don't hit a long ball, you may want to use one of the intermediate tees, which will give you a challenge without causing you the frustration of trying to hit the ball farther than you are capable.

Of course, there are more decisions involved in course strategy than which tee box to use. Where do you want to tee your ball within the tee box? From what position do you wish to hit your next shot? How far should you hit your tee shot or subsequent shots? What club do you use to hit your tee shot? What kind of shot do you want to hit? My goal in this chapter is to tell you something about how a golf hole is designed to challenge a golfer and how you can meet that challenge through strategic planning.

DESIGNING A GOLF COURSE

If you were to design a golf course, what components would you want to include? Perhaps to answer this question, we need to ask another question: why do people play golf? There are a variety of reasons.

❑ Socialization—Many golfers play golf to socialize. Almost any golf hole on any course provides us with the opportunity to interact with our friends or with someone we have just met.

❑ Fun and excitement—Golf is fun. It provides many opportunities for amusement, enjoyment, and entertainment, for humorous remarks and jokes. Laughter is the best method to manage stress. Many people who must be totally serious in their business or professional lives often allow themselves to reveal their other side on the golf course.

❑ Relaxation—Have you ever felt the need to get away from it all? To escape from the pressures of everyday life? You can get away from it all by concentrating on your golf game, by planning strategy for each hole and planning short strokes around the green. While you are playing golf, it is difficult for you to be preoccupied with other matters.

❑ Challenges—Golf challenges us to improve our skills, to think, and to solve problems.

❑ Competition—Golf invites us to play better than we did before, to play better than our opponents, to "beat" the course.

No matter why you play golf, you must be able to derive some satisfaction from playing the game. So, armed with the reasons why people play golf, how should we design a golf course? Here's how I would do it.

❑ I would pick an area with aesthetic beauty. I would want to look beyond the fairway to see mountains or a valley, trees, flowers, and birds. I want to be able to see and hear nature.

❑ I would lay out the hole so that it draws from my mental as well as my physical skills. I want the design to require me to use my head. Where do I want to hit my tee shot? How far do I hit the golf ball? What club do I use?

❑ I would place a few hazards outside the landing area to keep me thinking and to challenge my physical skills (golf fundamentals). Perhaps out-of-bounds on one side and trees on the other.

❑ I would bend the fairway so that it requires more thought on club selection from the tee and from the fairway. I would vary my design so that I would have to select a 3 wood off the tee followed by a 2 iron into the green on one hole and a driver and a 7 iron on another hole. I want the holes to be new, interesting experiences.

❑ I would put a sand bunker on the left and right corners of the fairway about 200 yards to help motivate me to hit a straight shot or to remind me to play my fade from left of the fairway to the middle of the fairway.

❑ I would place a couple of sand bunkers around the green, especially in front of my planned pin placements, to frustrate poor decisions. Perhaps a hill or drop off to the side where the ball of a less skilled golfer would go or the ball of a more skilled player trying to push his or her abilities. Perhaps a hazard to frustrate the long ball hitter who is not very accurate or who is trying to reach the green of a par five in two.

❑ I would elevate some tees and greens so that I would need to take elevation into account in my club selection.

These design steps would fill the requirements of most golfers who want an interesting round of golf. The course would be challenging, fun, and exciting and would stimulate players to solve problems, to be competitive, and to be creative. It would provide them with a lot of satisfaction, which, after all, is why most people play golf. Isn't that why you play?

Are you beginning to understand what this game is all about? Good! The next time you play golf, look at each hole from this new perspective. See the sand bunkers, the trees, the out-of-bounds stakes as the challenges of a well-thought-out design. The holes are not designed to "trap" you but to provide you with maximum enjoyment. Look back at the tee from your drive, look back at the fairway from the green. You will be surprised at what you see.

DECIDING ON A STRATEGY FOR THE HOLE

Most golf courses provide you with a descriptive diagram of every hole. It may appear on the score card or on the tee itself. The diagram will tell you if the hole is straight or a dogleg left or right and will help you to plan your strategy for playing the hole. Some diagrams have an ideal shot pattern indicated on the sketch or model advising you where to play your drive, second shot, and, on par 5's, third shot. If the diagram gives you the distance from the landing areas to the green, it is a matter of simple arithmetic to determine which club to use from the tee. Sometimes you are given only the minimum information, like Hole #10, 407 yards, par 4. How do you plan your strategy? Let's take a look at a hole from each of two different golf courses.

1. The number-two hole at Wyoming Valley Country Club

When I lived in Wilkes-Barre, Pennsylvania, I played golf at the Wyoming Valley Country Club. The number-two hole is a 90-degree dogleg left. The scorecard provides the following information: Hole #2, 338 yards, par 4, handicap 12.

Since you have probably never seen this course, why don't you use your imagination while I describe it. Put yourself on the #2 tee as if you were going to play the hole. When you stand on the tee, you can see that the hole is a severe dogleg left, but you cannot see the green. From where you are you can tell this much: The tee is elevated about ten to fifteen yards above the landing area with dense woods on the left, right, and back. The landing area is flat and begins to slope down at the extreme left (toward the green) and up at the back and right.

Having made par on #1, you have honors. You state, "It would be nice to know a little more about this hole before I tee off."

What information would help you in deciding how to hit your tee shot? Put a check mark next to the numbers that apply.

_____ 1. "I don't want to know anything—just give me my driver. This hole isn't the rest of my life."

_____ 2. Who was the sadist who designed this hole?

_____ 3. How can I gracefully replace this brand-new ball with one in my bag that I wouldn't mind losing?

_____ 4. Where are the out-of-bounds stakes?

_____ 5. How far is it to the middle (front-to-back) of the landing area?

_____ 6. What club will get me to the middle of the landing area?

_____ 7. What is my ball flight pattern for a club that can get me to the middle of the landing area?

_____ 8. Is my ball trajectory pattern important in hitting from this tee?

_____ 9. How far is it from the middle of the landing area to the green?

_____ 10. What is the elevation of the green in relation to the landing area?

_____ 11. From where in the landing area am I most likely to hit the green?

_____ 12. Where is the green?

_____ 13. Where is the pin?

_____ 14. Do I keep my left arm straight or my head down?

One of the members of your foursome (not your partner) volunteers, "You don't want to be long on your drive, that's for sure." His partner chimes in, "From the way you played number one, I'd hit a 2 iron all the way." I could devote the rest of this book to these two statements, but since we are on course strategy, I'll let them speak for themselves.

Meanwhile, your partner gives you this information:

❑ The shortest distance to the fairway is 155 yards, and the longest distance is 190 yards. You have already determined that the landing area left-to-right is about 85 yards.

❑ The small green is elevated about 10 yards above the landing area. It is trapped on the left with a sharp drop off to the right and back. The left part of the landing area is about 110 yards from the green, and the right landing is about 165 yards.

Are you ready to tee off? Perhaps. What do you know about the hole? List it below:

1. _____

2. _____

3. _____

4. _____

5. _____

Do you want any other information? No? Do you know if the landing area is wet or dry? Do you need to know that? What do you know about your swing? Circle or fill in what is appropriate:

❑ My ball flight pattern is (circle one)
   a) Straight, b) Right-to-left, or c) Left-to-right.

❑ I can use a (circle more than one)
   2 iron, 3 iron, 3 wood, 4 wood, 5 wood, or driver
   from this tee because I hit my (fill in)

2 iron	_____	yards
3 iron	_____	yards
5 wood	_____	yards
4 wood	_____	yards
3 wood	_____	yards
driver	_____	yards

Are you ready to tee off now? How much roll do you get with, say, your 3 wood? Is that important? It is if the fairway is dry and the grass cut short.

O.K. Let's play golf! You have determined that the best landing area from the white (intermediate) tee marker is about 175 yards. The tee marker is 4 yards behind the yardage marker, making your yardage to the best landing area 179 yards, with the front boundary of the landing area now 159 yards away and the back boundary of the landing area now 199 yards. A golfer would play this hole differently depending on many factors, one of which is his ball flight pattern (straight, left-to-right, or right-to-left). Since ball flight pattern is important, I'm going to walk you through each of these ball flight patterns using the number two hole. See figure 1 for a sketch of this hole.

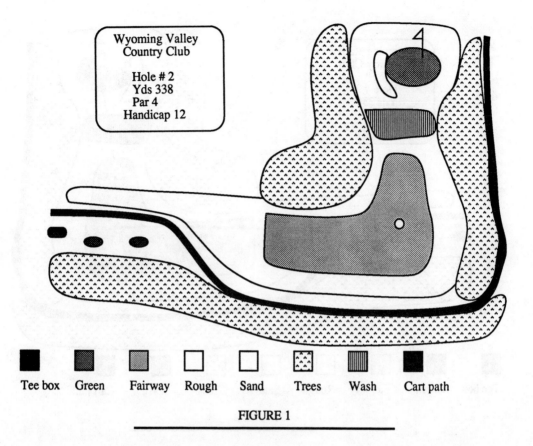

Tee box   Green   Fairway   Rough   Sand   Trees   Wash   Cart path

FIGURE 1

Number-two hole, Wyoming Valley Country Club
Ball flight pattern: *Left-to-right*
Let's say that your ball flight pattern is left-to-right 85 percent of the time and that you hit a 3 wood 200 yards 85 percent of the time (the other 15 percent you hit it 190 yards). Your distance with a 5 wood is 180 yards, 170 yards with a 3 iron, and 160 yards with a 4 iron. You don't have a 4 wood or a 2 iron. The fairway is neither excessively wet nor excessively dry, and the wind is not a factor off the tee.

You are hitting from an elevated tee and know that your shot will carry a little bit farther, but you don't know how much farther. Your club choices are to hit a 5 wood, a 3 iron, or a 4 iron. You think a 5 wood would put you too far. You can hit the 4 iron and try to get an additional nineteen yards. Since you will get about ten additional yards because of the elevated tee, you really only have to get an additional nine yards. The thought of this choice makes you tense. "What if I hit the ball fat?" "What if I'm short?" Your other choice is to use a 3 iron and take a relaxed swing knowing that you can easily get 180 yards (170 + 10 for elevation). But there

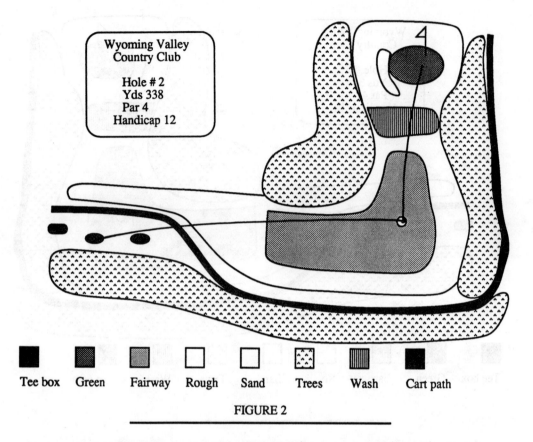

Wyoming Valley
Country Club

Hole # 2
Yds 338
Par 4
Handicap 12

| Tee box | Green | Fairway | Rough | Sand | Trees | Wash | Cart path |

FIGURE 2

is some doubt with this selection. The doubt is that you may hit it too far, that you may carry more than ten additional yards. Before you can execute your best shot, you must remove all doubt about the shot.

Let's look at the pitfalls of each choice and then decide. If you use the 4 iron thinking that you are really going to have to "nail it" to get it out there 179 yards, you may not even hit it past the forward tee. On the other hand, if you use the 3 iron and take a good swing, the worst that could happen is that you hit it farther than the 179 yards to the ideal landing area. Are you leaning toward the 3 iron?

Let's evaluate two more factors. The first is landing 189 yards away from the tee box. Landing 189 yards still leaves you within the fairway boundary. Is this a problem? Well, no. In the beginning of this simulation I assumed that you were a left-to-right player. In this case, your target is to a green with more trouble on the right than on the left. Would you like to hit your approach shot from the left fairway or from the right fairway? The optimal shot with your shot pattern is from the right part of the fairway: aim at the left trap and fade the ball onto the green. This way you are using all your strengths. You will still have a flat-to-slightly-sidehill stance, which is not a problem.

Are you ready? I think so. All you must decide is where to aim so that your ball lands at a distance from the green that would allow you to use a club you're confident about. If you aim down the middle of the fairway and fade the ball, you may have to use a long iron to the green. Worse, you may have to use a wood, which would be more difficult to aim and more difficult to hold the green if you hit it. So you will want to aim slightly left of center and work the ball back to center. Take a minute and mentally execute your golf shot. Perfect. See figure 2.

Number-two hole, Wyoming Valley Country Club
Ball flight pattern: *Straight*
This time, let's assume that you hit the golf ball relatively straight and about the same distance as in the first example. You have two decisions to make: what club do you use and where do you aim? On your approach shot to the green, you would like to be in the middle of the landing area, front-to-back, which is the middle of the fairway going into the green. Since you hit the ball straight, this will give you the best chance of hitting to the green where the pin is placed.

Which club will you use? The risk with the 4 iron is in hitting it short and

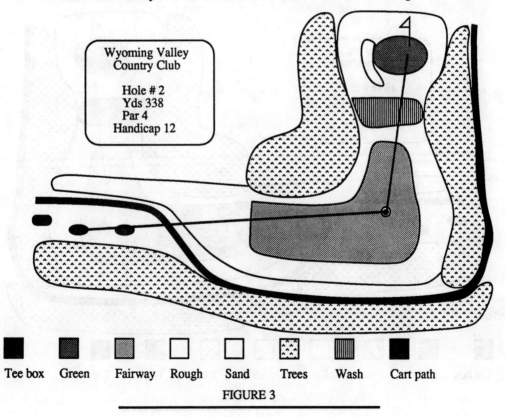

Wyoming Valley
Country Club

Hole # 2
Yds 338
Par 4
Handicap 12

Tee box   Green   Fairway   Rough   Sand   Trees   Wash   Cart path

FIGURE 3

blocking out a chance to go for the green. With a 3 iron, the risk is to hit it too long, which would either block out the right half of the green or give you a slightly sidehill lie. So you choose to use a 3 iron with a relaxed swing. Take a moment to visualize this shot. Your golf shot lands in the very target area that you visualized. See figure 3.

Number-two hole, Wyoming Valley Country Club
Ball flight pattern: *Right-to-left*
With a right-to-left ball flight pattern, you probably get about an additional ten yards with your woods. By aiming down the middle (a more reliable shot) and drawing the ball, you can get it to land in an area from which you can use a short iron to the green. A short-iron distance is desirable because it gives you a good opportunity to go for the small green with a more accurate club. See figure 4.

The #18 Hole at Ventana Canyon
The Canyon Course at Ventana Canyon Resort in Tucson, Arizona, is a typical desert course. Lush fairways, deep rough, and a lot of desert. Most holes have a

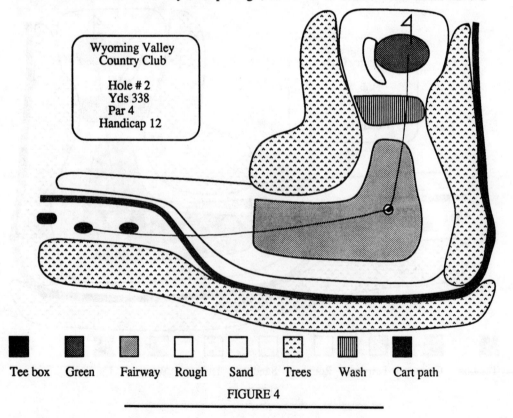

Wyoming Valley
Country Club

Hole # 2
Yds 338
Par 4
Handicap 12

| Tee box | Green | Fairway | Rough | Sand | Trees | Wash | Cart path |

FIGURE 4

desert landscape between the tee and the fairway. What is nice about playing Ventana is that, along with a scorecard, you get a booklet that pictures and describes each hole. The booklet is similar to what the touring pros look through before they hit their fairway shots. Suggested landing areas are indicated by bull's eyes, and there are ample yardage markers on the course as well as in the booklet. The scorecard does not suggest a tee box based on your handicap but does give you a rating as follows (par is 72):

Tees played:	**Copper**	**Silver**	**Gold**	**Black**
Course rating:	69.3	68.9	71.3	74.0
Tee description:	Forward	Intermed	Regular	Champ

The #18 hole at Ventana is 477 yards (Gold tees), par 5, handicap 12. There is some desert area between the tee box and the landing area, with little rough and a lot of desert to the left and to the right. The fairway narrows in the proposed landing areas. On the approach to the green is the Ventana Wash (so-called because there is usually no water in it). There is water behind and to the right of the green. The green, which is further guarded by a sand bunker to the left, is 72 yards deep and 65 yards wide.

This hole presents two special challenges. If you hit a long drive you may be tempted to go for the green in two, and if you are going to play finesse golf, you must decide what club to use on your second shot to set yourself up for your approach shot. See figure 5 for a sketch of this hole.

O.K. You are on the gold tees with a fairly strong wind behind you. You hit your tee shot with your driver—one of your best shots ever. When you get to your ball you discover that you drove it 250 yards. Wow! This leaves "only" 227 yards to the green. The thought that comes to your mind is, "Well, if I hit the driver 250 yards, I can certainly hit 227 yards with the 3 wood, especially with this tail wind. An eagle!" Then you think, "On the other hand, I could hit to the landing area before the wash, leave myself a 7 or 8 iron to the green, and put it close enough for a birdie attempt." Your best percentage club is your 7 iron. What are you going to do? You look again at the booklet describing the hole. The green is 65 yards wide and 72 yards deep. You can see the Ventana Wash in the picture. The booklet tells you that you "must carry" the wash with your approach shot. You notice the water behind and to the right of the green. You discount the trap on the left of the green, which is a lot less intimidating than the water or the wash. What is your best shot here? If you hit a perfect 3 wood, can you stop it on the green fast enough? Is an eagle try important enough to risk a six or seven? What is the worst that could happen? You think, "I could go in the water!" But, then you reflect, "I always lay up and still only make bogeys." If you lay up with a 9 iron (102 yards) and then go to

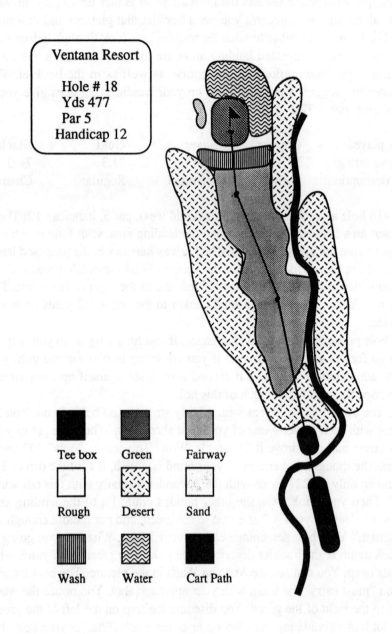

Ventana Resort

Hole # 18
Yds 477
Par 5
Handicap 12

Tee box   Green   Fairway

Rough   Desert   Sand

Wash   Water   Cart Path

FIGURE 5

the green with a 7 iron (130 yards), you can probably put it close enough for a birdie attempt or, at worst, a par.

You know that the fairway begins to slope down severely as you approach the wash. At the 130-yard mark, you have a flat lie and a good chance to hit a great golf shot.

Intelligence and reality prevail and you decide to hit a 9 iron to position yourself for the 7 iron shot to the green. You successfully hit the 9 iron 100 yards followed by the 7 iron (130 yards) just behind the pin. You one-putt for a birdie. Great way to finish a round and a great way to finish the chapter on strategy.

Since developing strategy is very important, I want to summarize the steps in descending order of the thought process:

❑ Length of the hole

❑ Hazard location

❑ Pin location on the green

❑ Prevailing conditions—weather and course

❑ Individual's predictable shot pattern and ability

❑ Positioning on the tee

❑ Pre-swing routine

SKULL PRACTICE: LEARNING THE MENTAL SKILLS
SELF-ESTEEM AND SPORT

> One of Muhammad Ali's colleagues, irritated by Ali's perpetual boasts of "I am the greatest," asked the boxer what he was like at golf. "I'm the best," replied Ali. "I just haven't played yet."

Belief in yourself is an essential ingredient for success, whether in your career, your health, or the sport you play. If you believe in yourself, you can accomplish whatever you desire. Ali believed in himself. It certainly paved the way for a successful career.

What is self-esteem? Self-esteem is that deep-down feeling that you are worthwhile. It is a voice that whispers, "You can do it" even when everyone around you is telling you it's impossible. Self-esteem is having positive thoughts and positive feelings about yourself overall. "I am O.K.," I am competent," "I can figure things out," "I am special," and "I can take care of myself." These statements mean healthy self-esteem.

Everyone is born with high self-esteem. As we grow up, if we're fortunate, we are accepted unconditionally by those around us. Parents and relatives give us many positive strokes, including plenty of attention and encouragement.

Some children are not so lucky. They are criticized and chastised by their parents, siblings, teachers, and peers. While some of the criticism and chastisement is motivated by good intentions, it has the net result of lowering self-esteem. These children are given the message that their worth is conditional. "Be a good boy and . . ." is a good example. There are other messages, like "Why can't you be like your sister?" "You're just like your father, you never do anything right!" or "Don't do that, you dummy!"

If you think our experiences growing up do not affect how we approach golf, listen to the way some people talk during a round of golf. When they miss a putt, they will call themselves "stupid" or "dummy." I often hear a golfer say, "Hit it, dummy!" It is as if someone told such people that they were dummies, they believed that they were dummies, and they now need to keep calling themselves "dummy" to reinforce what they have learned to believe.

There are more subtle ways of expressing the expectation of failure. A golfer hits a shot to the green, and as soon as the ball leaves the club, she will say, "It's in the trap!" This golfer is expecting the worst instead of waiting to see what happens. Interesting, the ball lands on the green most of the time. Another golfer focuses on a negative statement. As he makes an uphill putt he says out loud, "Don't leave it short."

People who have high self-esteem reflect contentment, confidence, capability, significance, love, respect, competence, and effectiveness.

But how do you get it if you don't have it? Self-esteem is a learned behavior. When someone is attempting to lower your self-esteem, realize that you are in charge of your life and that you are a competent and worthwhile person. If someone tries to do a psyche job on you by telling you that you are playing over your head, recognize the game that *he or she* is playing, smile, and concentrate on your own golf game.

INTEGRATION EXERCISES: GETTING YOUR MIND AND BODY TO WORK AS A UNIT

Exercises to improve course strategy

❑ Target areas. Draw a picture of a hole on your home course on which you usually have difficulty making par. Mark the total yardage, using figure 1 or figure 5 as a guide. Select an appropriate club for your tee shot. Indicate your proposed landing area with a circle and determine the yardage that you might drive the ball. Subtract this yardage from the total yardage and determine your distance to the green. Select a club that will get you to the target area on the green and decide if you can 2-putt from there. Your next step is to generate possibilities for each shot in your plan. For example, let's say you are very confident when you use your 6 iron from 150 yards. On a par 5, you may decide to use your driver from the tee and then a 4 iron to put you into position to use your 6 iron from 150 yards irons instead of a driver, a 3 wood, and a pitching wedge. The next time you play golf, try one of these options. If you like the way this approach works, follow it with the other holes.

❏ Walk your course. Some day when you are not going to play golf, take a walk around your course and observe the landing areas that are suitable for you. Take a look back at the tee. Take a look back to the fairway from the green. Take notes about what you learn.

Exercises to improve self-esteem*

❏ Like-list. List what you like about yourself. Don't be shy. Fill in a complete sheet of paper and use more sheets if necessary. You might include in your list that you are a good listener or that you are caring or that you are organized.

❏ Unique list. List what makes you unique. We all share many qualities and traits. Your particular pattern or combination of qualities and traits make you unique. For instance, you may have an interesting way of expressing yourself.

❏ Success list. List your successes. If you have lived to your teenage years, you have enough successes to fill several sheets of paper. Take your time and list each success you have had. You may have accomplished a college degree, or perhaps you are able to cook a really great meal.

---

* In my workshops I always have participants make three lists to help them to get a good perspective on their self-esteem. I can't overemphasize the importance of this drill in relation to your approach to learning golf and your approach to playing your best. Take a few minutes and work on these lists. Add liberally to them over time.

SECTION B

GETTING DOWN TO BASICS: LAYING
THE FOUNDATION

In chapter 1, you learned how to prepare to play golf, from what to do on the day before you play to what to do prior to play. Chapter 2 addressed how to navigate the course by developing a course strategy and a plan for each hole.

The purpose for putting these chapters in the beginning of the book was threefold. By knowing how to approach your golf match, you could immediately lower your score. By knowing how to plan the hole, you could instantly save strokes by playing smarter golf. By learning to use your head as well as your muscles, you could maximize your golf performance.

In the next two chapters I will teach you how to be consistent and predictable, two prerequisites for lowering your handicap, playing well, and having fun. Chapter 3 will help you to develop a pre-shot routine—what you do just prior to swinging your golf club or stroking your putter. Chapter 4 will help you to understand timing, the cornerstone of any sport. Again, the chapters are divided into three sections: Golf Fundamentals, Mental Skills, and Integration Exercises. Although I have included many exercises in the Integration Exercises sections, you don't need to do all of them as part of reading each chapter. Pick and choose to match your needs.

CHAPTER 3:

GETTING ORGANIZED: THE

PRE-SHOT ROUTINE

"In golf, you can never think too far ahead—not even
to the next hole. It is very important to work on the
shot you are on, not 'I can birdie the 15th hole' when
you are still trying to par the fifth. Patty Berg told me
once, 'Never think behind you or too far in front.
Never think of the bad hole that you just had; just
concentrate on the hole you are playing'."

— *Donna Caponi*
Professional Golfer

In the first chapter I asked you to identify and assess your daily activities the day
before and the day of your match. Activities to identify for the day before your
match included what you ate, what work you did, what your plan was for the next
day, when you went to sleep, and what relaxation techniques you would use. Activities to identify for the day of the match were what time you would awaken, how
you were to awaken, what you would eat for breakfast, how you would carry out
your planned activities for the day, how you would fill in your time before the
match, at what pace you would accomplish these activities, and how you would
warm up.

This was a lot to identify and a lot to evaluate. If you did your homework and
made a list of your activities, congratulate yourself on being a self-starter who is
motivated, self-disciplined, and well organized. If you didn't, don't be upset, you
can do it now. It's not too late!

I think it is important to identify the thoughts and feelings you had when you

53

decided not to do the exercises. When you made your decision not to write out your daily routine, not to write out your plan of activities, and not to write out your warmup routine, did you decide not to do it because (circle the phrase that fits best)

a) "Who has time for lists? I need to read this book before the weekend."
b) "It's not important to list these things."
c) "I don't have to write these things down in order to learn."
d) "This is kid's stuff; it's stupid to write things down like this.
e) "I just want to read a book and get better—I really don't want to do too much work."
f) "I just didn't get around to it yet."

If you chose a) "Who has time?", I can empathize, because I can understand how excited and enthusiastic you might be about improving your golf game. But patience and hard work—in the form of time and effort—are the keys to learning and improving any skill. Have you ever had a chip shot around the green and decided to hit it without a couple of practice swings? Choice a) is the same thing as hitting the chip shot without a practice shot. If you want to be your very best, I suggest that you take the time now and learn from the exercise. We will be building a foundation that, when the chips are down, will get you out of trouble every time. Go ahead, do the exercise; I'll wait. Remember, if you don't have time to do it right the first time, when will you find the time to do it again?

If you chose b) "It's not important", I have a question for you. Do you sometimes find yourself on the course with the wrong club in your hand and think, "I'm not going back to the cart to get another club; I can get away with hitting this one . . . ?" Or have you ever been in a situation where you are ready to hit your approach shot to the green and think: "I didn't look to see if the pin is placed in back or to the front . . . Oh well, it doesn't matter . . ?" If you have, we are going to have to do a little more work on mental effort. If you really intend to improve your golf game— and I suspect you do or you wouldn't have bought this book—you will need to perform some tasks that may at first seem unimportant. They will reveal their importance further down the road.

If you chose c) "I don't have to write to learn", you should know that according scientific research we learn better when we use all of our senses. If we want to learn something, we can increase our efficiency of learning if we can see it, hear it, or write it. We are most effective when we do all three.

If you chose d) "This is kid's stuff", all I can say is that when any of us learn a new skill or want to improve what we have learned, we need to go back to the basics—back to the "kindergarten" of our skill to check out what we know and what we do not know. When I interviewed touring professional golfers, I asked them, "What do you do when you get in trouble?" All of them, PGA and LPGA, answered that they look to their fundamentals—grip, posture, and stance. They don't think it's kid's stuff.

If you chose e) "I don't want to do too much work", read the second-to-last paragraph again. You cannot learn without doing some work. It is like the patient who goes to the doctor with a lifestyle problem, like being overweight or addicted to smoking, and asks for a pill instead of a plan to solve his or her problem.

If you chose f) "Didn't get around to it yet", now's the time, while there are only a few exercises to do. Later, if you get overwhelmed, you may quit. This won't do you any good, and it certainly won't speak very highly of my ability to motivate you to learn better golf. You'll tell your friends, "I bought Fasciana's book and it didn't help."

Preview of chapter 3

In this chapter I want to teach you how to develop a pre-shot routine that will help you on every shot from the putter to the driver, whether your golf swing is a full or a partial swing, whether you have executed the shot hundreds of times before or will execute it for the first time. Some elements of the pre-shot routine you will easily do from experience. Others may require you to read other sections of the book before you try them. For example, visualization—forming a mental image of the ball going into the hole on a six-to-eight-foot putt—is something that will help improve your putting. If you want to improve your putting you will need to learn this valuable mental tool.

You will also build on what you have learned in chapter 2 about course strategy. Chapter 2 led you into an *active mode* while on the golf course. Being an active golfer— one who thinks and evaluates while on the course but who can shift into auto-pilot during the swing itself—is important to achieve maximum golf performance.

GETTING ORGANIZED

The pre-shot routine may be *the* most important step you take in golf. Why? It does for you what any routine provides: *allows you perform automatically without conscious thought*. This will help you to play better by allowing you to swing and putt subconsciously while consciously focusing on what you want to accomplish. An exact, repeatable sequence of actions puts you in the same position every time. Being in the exact position each time creates feelings of comfort.

An automatic routine has mental benefits that include quieting your mind and reducing tension and anxiety. You begin to think about the process of getting from point A to point B instead of thinking about golf mechanics, the consequences of the shot, or the outcome of the tournament. A pre-shot routine also increases your alertness and attention, both of which help you to *feel* the golf shot. This feeling promotes a sense of timing, rhythm, and pace. The pre-shot routine is the bridge between conscious thought about the shot and subconscious execution of the golf shot.

Awareness of fundamentals: your pre-shot routine
Do you know your pre-shot routine? If you don't, take a few minutes to learn what it is. First, think about what you do before you make your golf shot. Write this down in sequence. Next, get a golf club and a golf ball and go into the back yard. Place the ball on the ground and do everything that you do when you are going to hit a golf shot. Sometimes having someone there is helpful. Your partner can take notes of what you are doing, and you can then return the favor. A video camera is an especially helpful tool. Is there a relationship between what you thought you did and what you actually did?

The pre-shot routine
I am going to describe the process of getting the golf ball from point A (the tee) to point B (the landing area). Each step is a part of what is called the pre-shot routine.*
The twelve-step pre-shot routine is as follows.

Standing behind the ball
(Ball is between you and the target)

1. **Environmental assessment.** You need to put some basic information into your mental computer before executing any golf shot. This information includes data about the landing area, data about the lie of the ball, and wind conditions. Some of the following questions will be more or less important, depending on whether you are on the tee hitting to a fairway or in the fairway hitting to a green. The important data to evaluate is:

   ❏ Landing Area
   How far is it to where I want the golf ball to land?
   Is there anything in the way—trees, sand, water?
   Is the landing area flat or sloping?
   Am I higher or lower than the landing area?

   ❏ Lie of the golf ball
   How thick is the grass beneath the ball?
   How deep is the ball buried in the grass?

---

* This description of a pre-shot routine is fairly detailed. Some golfers use all of these steps, while others select those that are important to them. The more precise your routine is however, the more success you will have. Experiment and find out what steps are important for your game.

Am I swinging against or with the grain of the grass?
Is the grass wet?
Is the ball above or below my feet?
Do I have a sidehill, uphill, or downhill lie?

❑ Wind conditions
Is the flag moving? How much?
Are the branches on the trees in the landing area moving?
What is the direction of the wind?

2. **Target.** The first decision is, where you want the golf ball to land? The part of the fairway or the green where the ball is to land is called the target area.

3. **Target Line.** There is an invisible line from the golf ball to the target area called the target line. It could be straight or curved. If it is curved, it could be curved left-to-right or right-to-left, depending on the ball flight pattern you intend to use. Once you decide how you want to get the ball to the target, "see" the target line. If you want to hit the golf ball straight, "see" a straight line; if you want the ball to go right-to-left (draw), "see" a curved line going from right-to-left; and if you want the ball to go left-to-right (fade), "see" a curved line going from left-to-right.

    Standing at about the 7 o'clock position, you should be able to "see" a line going from the ball to your intended target. This line will guide you in aiming the clubface toward the target and will help you to align yourself along that line.

4. **Visualize your shot.** You have a target and a line over which your golf ball will travel. You have decided on your ball flight pattern. Your next step is to "see" the ball go from where it is sitting to the landing area. During this step, what you see is what you get. "Watch" the ball leave the ground; notice the trajectory. Notice the curve of the ball in flight. Watch the ball land. Watch it roll to a stop. When the golf ball landed, did it go straight, left, or right? If you are a left- to-right hitter, you should see the ball land and then go slightly right depending on the club you are using.

    Once you have previewed the flight of your golf shot, you may want to take a mini-swing to integrate the picture of the ball flight and the swing you must take to convert your visualized shot into a reality. You may want to attach a swing cue or a feeling to the swing to help you to execute your shot. Take as many preview swings as necessary for you to have the right feel for what you are about to accomplish.

5. **Programming swing (stroke).** To integrate your visualization of your golf shot with the effort needed to accomplish your golf shot, you need to

program your muscles. This programming takes place in one of three forms: programming the exact stroke, programming the exact swing, or programming for timing or tempo.

Programming the exact stroke is used for chipping and putting. In chipping, you want to program the exact stroke required to drop the ball to your target area. In putting, you want to program the exact effort and movement required to roll the golf ball to the center of the cup.

Programming the exact swing is also used for any other swing that is less than a full swing, such as pitching the ball to the green from forty yards. If you decide on a 9 o'clock pitching wedge, you need to program that shot before you proceed with your pre-shot routine.

In a full swing, programming for timing is used. It is not your intention to program the exact golf swing but to give your muscles cues so that your movements occur in the correct sequence at the correct time. The program for timing looks like a mini-swing, and that is exactly what it is.

6. **Pick an intermediate target.** Except for the shortest putt, your target will be beyond your peripheral vision when you address the ball. An intermediate target, approximately three-to-eight feet in front of you, will help you to establish the line of the golf shot without having to see the target and the ball simultaneously. This target line will also help guide your swing so that you swing on the correct path and the golf ball travels along your intended line. An intermediate target could be a tee, a divot, a leaf, or anything that you can identify and use for alignment. The tee box gives you an opportunity to place your ball anywhere between the tee markers. Take advantage of this opportunity and tee up your ball behind a divot, a clump of grass, or some other object.

Standing on the side of the ball
(You are standing perpendicular to the target line)

7. **Aim the clubface.** Aiming the club usually goes like this. From the eight o'clock position, aim the clubface down the target line and at the intermediate target. Position your right foot perpendicular to the target line, position your left foot perpendicular to the target line, grip the club, and reposition your body.

You may have a slightly different sequence of aiming the club. If you don't have a routine for this, you should develop one. Notice that in my description your address position is built around the target line, first by aiming the clubface, then by aligning your body, then by gripping the golf club. If you grip the club first, you may turn your hands to "square-up" the club. Then, when you swing, your hands will return to the position you had before you turned your hands, and the clubface will no longer be square.

8. **Get comfortable.** Move your feet or your arms slightly or whatever you need to move to get yourself comfortable. Most of the discomfort at this point arises from tension or rigidity in your setup—grip, stance, posture. If you are not aligned correctly, you may feel awkward. If you feel awkward, start again.

9. **Do a body scan.** A body scan identifies any areas of your body that are holding unnecessary tension. Start with your head and go through the different parts of your body. I'll say more about this in the chapter on stress management. Once you have identified those parts of your body that are tense, relax them. Unnecessary tension will adversely affect your setup, swing plane, and power transfer, resulting in an ineffective shot.

The Execution of the Golf Shot

10. **Waggle the club.** The waggle is the bridge between the address position and the actual start of the golf swing. It is a mini mini-swing—a preview, or "dry run," as Hogan describes it, of what is to happen.

    The waggle sets the stage for the actual swing. During the waggle several things happen: you preview the *path* the club will take, you preview the *pace* at which you will swing, you *program the timing* of your swing, you *send the instructions* for creating the shot from your brain to your muscles, and you *adjust your setup* so that the club comes squarely through the ball when you take your golf swing.

    Obviously, the waggle varies from shot to shot, since it is a mini-swing of the shot you are creating, which changes in different situations. For instance, you may take a long, flowing waggle for a full swing on the tee and a shorter waggle for a 60-yard pitch shot.

11. **The forward press.** Although some teaching pros do not advocate the forward press, many do. If it is done correctly, it serves as a signal for your body to begin the sequences of movements called the golf swing. The forward press can consist of your right knee flexing slightly toward the left (like Gary Player) or a slight forward movement of your hands at the address position (like Jack Nicklaus). The forward press occurs just after the last waggle and just before the backswing.

12. **The swing.** After the forward press, you simply take the club back and let the swing happen as planned.

Using a Pre-shot Routine

Your pre-shot routine will be pretty much the same for most golf shots. Following is a summary of how the routines differ for each of the major shots.

❏ **Driver**—Because you are standing on a flat area and teeing the ball, the lie of the golf ball will be less important than the landing area and wind conditions. Your visualization of the shot will take a little bit longer, since the shot will travel farther and the ball flight pattern and trajectory will be those associated with the driver. In visualizing your drive, you will see the ball roll a greater distance than for other clubs.

❏ **Fairway woods and long irons**—With the fairway woods and the long irons, the lie of the ball and the ground where you are standing become important. Your visualization of the golf shot differs from that of the driver because your shot pattern is different. You will see less roll once the golf ball hits the ground or the green.

❏ **Short irons**—With the short irons, all parts of the pre-shot routine come into play—wind conditions to a greater or lesser extent than they did with the driver depending on your ball trajectory. In visualizing your golf shot, you will see the ball go higher and land softly on the green.

❏ **Putting, chipping, and pitching**—I will discuss shots around the green and putting separately in their respective chapters.

SKULL PRACTICE: LEARNING THE MENTAL SKILLS—GOAL SETTING

> "I'm working as hard as I can to get my life and my cash to run out at the same time. If I can just die after lunch Tuesday, everything will be perfect."
>
> — *Doug Sanders*
> Professional Golfer

If achievement is the destination, goal-setting is the road to get there. Many people are unsuccessful because they fail to set goals, or they set goals beyond their reach. Such goals are either too general or unrealistic in their present form. If I asked you to tell me your goal in golf and you replied, "To be a scratch golfer (your present handicap is 18)," I might have some serious doubts about whether you could achieve your goal. If you answered, "My goal is to become a scratch golfer in two years, and I'm presently working on taking two putts or fewer on every green," I would think you had a pretty good chance of meeting your goal.

What are goals? In golf, goal is achieving a specific standard of proficiency in a skill or a task within a specified period. Thus it contains two parts: a specific result and a time frame within which to produce that result. Why are goals important? Because they work. Goals help to determine what is important to you, maintain motivation, increase effort, direct attention, and increase the effectiveness of learning strategies. There are several kinds of goals, depending on your focus.

❑ Short-term goals are related to specific tasks (such as two-putting every green).

❑ A long-term goal is more general (lower your handicap five strokes by the end of the summer).

❑ Subjective goals raise your level of enjoyment or self-esteem (have fun while playing, or play relaxed).

❑ Objective goals are specific and can be measured (two-putting each green is an objective goal).

❑ Outcome goals are about results (winning the club championship).

❑ Performance goals are process-oriented. You could have a performance goal of following through on every shot. Athletes with performance goals have less worry and anxiety about their sport and generally perform well.

How important is goal-setting? One of the most highly researched findings in goal-setting is that proper goal-setting leads to improved performance. Setting appropriate goals reduces anxiety, increases confidence, and improves motivation. Goal-setting also directs your attention to develop specific skills, mobilizes your efforts, and increases your enthusiasm and motivation.

Guidelines for setting goals:

❑ Set goals that are specific and measurable, such as to hit 75 percent of the greens in regulation.

❑ Set difficult but realistic goals—challenging but attainable.

❑ Set short-term goals. This gives improved performance feedback, which enhances motivation, confidence, and enthusiasm. Short-term goals ultimately enable you to accomplish overall long-term goals.

❑ Set performance goals. These allow control and flexibility and keep your mind in the here and now.

❑ Set positive goals. Positive goals promote positive behavior. Make the statement, "I'm going to two-putt each green" rather than "Don't three-putt."

❑ Identify target dates for attaining goals. Target dates give urgency to accomplishing objectives while establishing a reasonable time frame.

❑ Record your goals. A record provides feedback about accomplishing your goals.

❑ Evaluate your goals. This allows you to change goals when appropriate.

❑ Provide support for your goals: share them with someone who can offer support to you when you need it.

INTEGRATION EXERCISES: GETTING YOUR MIND AND BODY TO WORK AS A UNIT

Exercises to improve golf fundamentals

1. **Pre-shot routine.** To identify your pre-shot routine, take a friend with you to the practice range and hit a few balls. Ask your friend to record the steps you make, from assessment of the shot through execution. You will want to do this exercise on the course as well. You may find that your routine in practice differs from your routine in play.

2. **Programming stroke.** Take a dozen golf balls to the practice green. Set yourself up for two-foot putts, four-foot putts, and six-foot putts. Determine how much effort it will take to make each putt and program your stroke.

3. **Programming swing.** Go to the practice range and get a bucket of golf balls. After warming up, hit several dozen golf balls using a pitching wedge. Hit some with a 9 o'clock backswing, a 10 o'clock backswing, and an 11 o'clock backswing.

4. **Programming for timing.** Go to the practice range and get a bucket of golf balls. After warming up, prepare to hit several 7 iron shots. Just prior to swinging, take your mini mini-swing to program for timing.

Exercises to improve goal-setting

1. Identifying goals. Write several examples of your short-term and long-term goals for your golf game.

2. Use the Goal-Setting Worksheet on the following page to set a short-term goal.

GOAL-SETTING WORKSHEET

A. "MY GOAL IS _____ "

B. "I will reach this goal on or before _____ "

C. I see the following *barriers* to achieving this goal:

1. _____

2. _____

3. _____

4. _____

5. _____

D. "I will *overcome* these barriers by doing the following:"

1. _____

2. _____

3. _____

4. _____

5. _____

E. "I will obtain the following *benefits* when I reach my goal:"

1. _____

2. _____

3. _____

4. _____

5. _____

F. "I am/am not willing to invest the time and effort necessary to obtain the benefits that achieving this goal will provide."

Signed: _____ Date: _____

CHAPTER 4:

EXECUTION: TIMING, RHYTHM,

AND PACE

> I try not to let anything interfere with my game plan. I know I need patience and I'm determined to maintain a good attitude. After all, that's the sign of a pro—keeping your cool. Look at those pro quarterbacks. They don't get flustered when they're behind with two minutes to go. They just keep their poise and let things happen.
>
> — *Tom Weiskopf*
> Professional Golfer

If we set out to drive from New York to Los Angeles, we would pass from one town to another. The process of passing from one place (point A) to another (point B) is called movement. We would move from point to point. Our car odometer would indicate the distance we had traveled. If we had a stop watch, we could keep track of the time that elapsed while driving. With these two pieces of information, we could calculate the average *rate* at which we traveled—distance (miles) divided by time (hours). This rate of movement is called *pace*. Pace tells how rapidly movement takes place.

Suppose we drove ten hours every day until we reached Los Angeles. This pattern of movement could be considered the rhythm of our journey. The regular occurrence of activity is called *rhythm*.

Let's take a look at how timing, rhythm, and pace relate to golf.

TIMING

Charlie Chaplin asked a playwright named MacArthur to write for him. The playwright soon ran into difficulties. "What's the problem?" asked Chaplin. MacArthur said, "How can I make a fat lady, walking down Fifth Avenue, slip on a banana peel and still get a laugh? It's been done a million times. What's the best way to get a laugh: Do I show first the banana peel, then the fat lady approaching, then she slips? Or, do I show the fat lady first, then the banana peel, and then she slips?"

"Neither," said Chaplin. "You show the fat lady approaching; then you show the banana peel; then you show the fat lady and the banana peel together; then she steps over the banana peel and disappears down a manhole."

What is timing?

Timing is defined as the moment at which each of a sequence of movements occurs. This is worth repeating: The moment at which each of a sequence of movements occurs. This definition implies that there are two or more movements, that these movements occur in a specific order, and that each movement occurs in time. On our imaginary trip from New York to Los Angeles, we went through various cities on our way, through Pittsburgh, Indianapolis, St. Louis, and so on. To complete our trip in an efficient manner, we needed to go through Pittsburgh, then through Indianapolis, and then through St. Louis. If we did not go through these cities in that order, our trip would take longer than necessary. The cost for such a travel plan is additional time, effort, and gasoline.

In golf, too, movements occur in a specific order. You must make certain movements before you make others. The golf swing, for example, consists of changing general positions from the address position to the at-the-top position of the backswing, then the downswing to the impact position, and finally to the finish position. In addition to these general position changes, there are specific ones. The backswing is initiated with your arms taking the club back. This movement is followed by a shoulder turn, then a hip turn, then a movement backward by your left knee, and, finally, by a movement of your left heel lifting off the ground. The reverse occurs with the forward swing. Each movement takes place in an exact sequence. Each movement takes place in time.

Why is timing important in the golf swing?

When golf movements take place in the correct sequence, maximum efficiency generates maximum power. No excess effort or energy is needed. "Effortless" energy is applied to the golf swing and the ball. The swing looks and feels effortless because the effort is shared by all the muscles involved. You don't feel you are swinging your arms too hard or turning your shoulders too fast.

If your golf movements do not take place in the correct sequence, your golf swing falls out of sync, resulting in loss of energy and a decline in performance. If, on your backswing, you were to start your hip turn first, your sequence would be incorrect. Your effort might be maximal, but your performance would be minimal. Maximal effort and minimal performance.

So to generate maximum power, specific muscles of your body must react in a specific order. Each part of the golf swing transfers energy to the next to build maximum energy. If some muscles are pushing and others pulling, the effort is great but the movement is small.

The essence of timing, then, is that each of a sequence of movements occurs in a specific order at a specific point in time.

TIMING ERRORS

These ordered sequences of movements will occur naturally when you allow them to, but many factors can interfere. Thus, when you have a problem with timing, you need to find out what was creating the interference and remove it. Only then will you allow your swing to take place by itself.

What can interfere with your natural movements? Some of the barriers to a well-timed golf swing fall into the following general categories.

❑ **Physical barriers**—General fatigue, muscular fatigue, poor physical fitness, lack of physical skills, muscular tension, and improper diet.

❑ **Mental barriers**—Mental fatigue, emotional distress, distractions, attitude, negative internal dialogue, and anxiety.

❑ **Playing outside yourself**—Trying to hit the ball too hard or too far, or attempting a miracle shot.

No matter what it is that interferes with your timing, the interference causes an alteration in the sequence of movements, reducing your efficiency and resulting in a less-than-perfect golf shot.

Let's say you are playing the #17, par 5 hole at the Greenville Country Club (Chanticleer) in Greenville, South Carolina. The seventeenth hole is a 497-yard, par 5 from the championship tees. There is water in front and to the left and right of the green. You tee off from the intermediate tee and hit an excellent drive that leaves you 225 yards from the green. You must carry 175 yards to get over the stream in front of the green. You know that you can carry your 3 wood 205 yards.

Let's assume the following:

❑ You are feeling energetic and not tired in any way. You feel some muscular tension when you think of hitting to the green from where you are.

❑ You feel fine mentally without any emotional distress or distractions. You

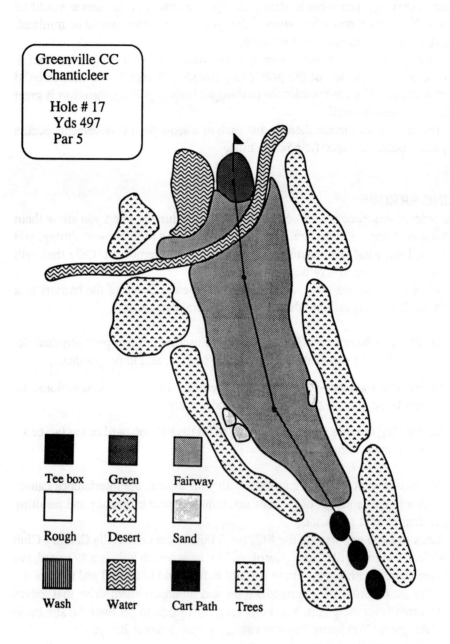

Greenville CC
Chanticleer

Hole # 17
Yds 497
Par 5

Tee box   Green   Fairway

Rough   Desert   Sand

Wash   Water   Cart Path   Trees

FIGURE 1

do feel some anxiety about going in the water if you don't hit your shot straight.

❑ You think you really have to hit the ball hard to put it on the green.

Any one of these three factors, muscular tension, anxiety, or thinking that you must hit the ball hard, far, or straight, can interfere with a full swing and compromise your shot-making ability. Muscular tension shortens the muscles needed to swing the club on its widest arc and at its maximum speed. Your efficiency and power will be reduced, making it less likely that you can hit the ball to where you intend. Anxiety about hitting the ball far or avoiding hitting into the water will further increase muscular tension; it will make you tight. You will probably swing too fast or put too much effort into one part of your swing, causing you to change the path of your swing, switch the order of movements, or shift the position of the clubface at impact. An example of how tension can interfere with a good golf swing is what many golfers do in an attempt to get more distance: they will "jump" on the ball and start their forward swing with their arms or shoulders, creating an outside-in swing plane. This is sometimes described as coming over the top and results in a fat shot, a pull, or a slice. Certainly not what the golfer intended.

PACE

Louis Mayer, a film producer, admired class and wanted badly to possess it. Told that golf was a classy sport, he at once took it up. But he never seemed to get the hang of it, never quite understood that it was scored in strokes. Instead he saw it as a kind of race. He employed *two* caddies. One caddy was posted down the fairway to locate the ball at once. Meanwhile caddy number two would run ahead, Mayer pelting behind him, to station himself for the next shot. The game over, Mayer would consult his watch. "We made it in one hour and seven minutes! Three minutes better than yesterday."*

What is pace?
Pace is the rate of movement—how fast a movement occurs. It is not to be confused with timing. In a short putt, the putter is taken back (backswing) and then stroked toward the hole (forward swing). More specifically, it begins going back, reaches the end of the backswing, changes direction, is stroked forward, makes contact with the ball, and finishes the forward stroke. Each of these movements takes place at a moment in time. How fast each occurs is called pace.

* *Anecdotes*, Fadiman, Little, Brown and Company, Boston.

Why is pace important in golf?

A full golf swing may take 3½ seconds from start to finish. Three-and-a-half seconds is the time it takes to swing the golf club back, change direction, and swing the golf club forward to the finish position.

This measurement tells you the total time it takes to swing the golf club. What it doesn't tell you is how much time you allocated to each specific part of the swing. For example, if your backswing took half a second and your forward swing took three seconds, would this be acceptable? Probably not. Your backswing would probably be too fast relative to the rest of your swing. What would be acceptable is a difficult question to answer in a general way.

It is more important for you to know your optimal pace, the pace at which you strike the ball with the least effort and the greatest result. Look at Nancy Lopez's swing. Her backswing is almost in slow motion. It works for her. Greg Norman's backswing is faster. It works for him. You need to experiment to determine what works for you.

You can learn more about your pace on a day when your goal is to practice timing. Timing is best learned with the simplest stroke: with a putter at a distance of four to five feet. Without using a golf ball, take the putter back very slowly, maintaining control, and slowly stroke it forward. Call this forward stroke speed number one. Still using a slow backstroke, take a slightly faster forward stroke and call this speed number two. Take a forward stroke that is a little faster than number two and call it number three. Continue this until you get to a number that represents the fastest speed at which you can control the putter.

The next thing you need to do to learn about your pace is to take the putter back at, say, one and forward at two. Then take the putter back at two and forward at three. Continue doing this until you get a feel for what speed is correct for you. You will know your optimal pace fairly easily.

When you have learned about your putting stroke, repeat this with one of your short irons. Then do the same with one of your mid-irons and work your way up to your driver. You may want to divide this practice into three or four practice sessions.

What are the consequences of getting out of pace? If your pace is faster than optimal, what happens? Do you hit the ball fat? Do you pull it left? Do you slice it? What happens when your pace is slower than optimal? Do you lose distance? Do you shank the ball?

Once you realize the importance of pace you must make a commitment to keep your pace in spite of what is going on around you. This may mean getting out of bed more slowly, eating breakfast more slowly, getting dressed more slowly, driving to the course more slowly, and warming up more slowly. It is difficult, if not impossible, for you to rush to the course and expect to calm down and play at a relaxed pace.

RHYTHM

What is rhythm?

Rhythm is the regular occurrence of the natural flow of movement. Rhythm is about consistency. When we think of consistent performance, we use words like dependable, reliable, solid, steady, sure, tried, and trustworthy to describe a golf swing or how a golfer plays.

Why is rhythm important in golf?

Ask yourself these questions. Do you consistently make five-foot putts? Are your shots to the green fairly consistent? Do you put most of your drives in the fairway? If the answer to these questions is yes, your rhythm is probably good. If the answer to these questions is no, then your rhythm could probably use some improvement.

An important characteristic of every low-handicap golfer is consistency. If lowering your handicap is your goal, you want to be able to swing your golf club the same way each time. Wouldn't it be nice to have your tee shot land in the fairway most of the time, to hit the green in regulation most of the time, to lag long putts within tap-in range, and to sink four-to-eight foot putts most of the time?

ESTABLISHING YOUR PACE ON DAYS WHEN YOU DON'T HAVE THE FEEL

O.K. It's the day of the shotgun tournament. You have been practicing your fundamentals and you've been hitting the ball as well as you ever have. You go to the driving range to warm up. You pull your first practice shot outside the driving range. You quickly put another ball down. This time you slice. You put another ball down, this time more quickly than the last ball. You swing and "chili-dip" it. You think, "Oh my God, what's happening to me?"

I often get asked, "How do I get the right timing when it just doesn't seem to be there?" One of the most common problems golfers have is that some days their timing is not just right and they can't seem to get it right during warmup. Panic sets, with rapid heart rate, elevated blood pressure, muscular tension, tightness in the chest, and a shutdown of the thought process. Before they know it, they are basket cases.

The simple solution is to have a good warm-up routine that incorporates several drills. Here is an example of what you might do.

❏ Begin the swing component of your routine with a few putting strokes without the ball. Feel the weight of the putter head.

❏ Putt a few long putts—15 to 20 footers to a one-foot circle on the green. Mark the circle with a few tees.

- ❏ Putt some 3-footers. Listen to how great it sounds when the golf ball drops in the cup.

- ❏ Putt some 4-footers. Then some 5-footers.

- ❏ Take a few chipping strokes without a ball. Feel the weight of the club-head. Get the feel for what it would take to get the ball to the hole.

- ❏ Chip a few balls.

- ❏ Go to the driving range and take some mid-iron shots. Work your way to the driver.

If this fails, do the pace drill using the speed of one, the speed of two, and so forth. The more you build from square one, the greater your chances of correcting the pace problem. Preventing the panic attack is easier than dealing with it once it happens because during a panic attack you are likely to generate some negative thoughts and feelings that take more work to overcome.

I've been playing long enough to know that I need to go to the practice pitching range once every two or three weeks if I want to maintain my tempo. First I practice a few 9 o'clock shots, then some 10 o'clock shots, then some 11 o'clock shots.* This routine reinforces my pace for my golf swing. During this practice I usually experience the golf ball exploding from the face of the club. It feels effortless. If I don't practice like this, I find myself pushing or forcing my swing instead of letting it happen. You too should experiment and find out what you need to do to maintain your tempo.

USING WEIGHTS TO LEARN THE FEEL OF A WELL-TIMED SWING

In the beginning of my golf career, on at least three or four occasions, I had a timing problem that resulted in a slice. I successfully corrected my slice by taking a "three-quarter" swing. Actually, when I videotaped my swing, I found that it was more a full swing than a three-quarter swing. It worked because when I took what I thought was a three-quarter swing, I didn't put pressure on myself to get back and through rapidly. I had assumed that if I swung fast, I would hit the ball farther, because a fast swing results in a higher clubhead speed—right? Maybe, but not likely. What the three-quarter swing did was slow down my pace to allow all the parts of my body to move in the correct sequence at the correct time. Timing—not speed and not strength—is the essential ingredient for distance and direction.

Now, with a few years under my belt, a few lessons, and a greater under-

---

* More about clock positions in chapter 7.

standing of the mental part of the golf swing, I have learned a weight drill that may help you to learn your ideal pace. You may want to practice this drill found at the end of the chapter, to improve your timing.

SKULL PRACTICE: LEARNING THE MENTAL SKILLS—THOUGHT CONTROL

> "If you think you can or you think you can't, you're always right."
>
> —*Henry Ford I*

Your ultimate success depends on your internal dialogue. If you whisper win messages, you will win; if you whisper lose messages, you will lose. It doesn't matter whether you are whispering about your personal life, business, health, or the sport you play.

I played golf with two men in their seventies. On a par 3, both men hit their tee shots in the fairway about 40 yards from the pin. The first golfer got his golf club out of his bag, said, "O.K. little feller, let's get on up there," and proceeded to hit his golf shot. The second golfer got his club out of his bag, said, "Now don't leave it short, whatever you do," and proceeded to hit *his* golf shot.

Predictably, one golf ball ended up one foot away from the pin, while the other landed about 25 feet short of the pin. I think you know which golfer was close to the pin. What you think is what you get! If you are thinking about what you *don't* want, you had better change your thoughts to what you do want before you swing your golf club. You'll get much better results.

How do our thoughts influence our behavior? They create what we feel about certain things. These feelings, in turn, generate our behavior. Our behavior reinforces what we think, and the cycle goes on. If you want to change this cycle, you need to intervene at some point and reprogram the cycle. A good place to start is with the negative thought. Identify what you are saying to yourself and learn to make your thoughts positive.

How to talk to yourself

How you feel about yourself (see chapter 2, self-esteem) determines what you tell yourself. What you tell yourself determines how you see yourself. How you see yourself determines how you deal with the situations life presents to you. For instance, do you see an event as a challenge or as a burden? Here are some guidelines for thought control.

1. Identify what you are saying to yourself. So much of what we say to ourselves is negative. If we are aware of this, we can do something about it.

2. Stop negative thoughts. Focus on the unwanted thought and use a *trigger* to stop it in its tracks. The trigger could be snapping your finger, saying the word "stop" to yourself, or any other cue that you believe can stop the thought. At times you may decide just to let negative thoughts pass through your mind without paying any attention to them.

3. Change negative thoughts to positive thoughts. For example, change "I don't know if I can make this down-hill putt" to "I am a good putter. I'm going to roll this one in the hole."

4. Counter. If you change a negative thought to a positive thought and you still believe the negative statement, you must do some additional exercises. An internal dialogue using facts, figures, and reason can refute the underlying beliefs and assumptions that led to the negative thought.

5. Reframe irrational thinking patterns.

   ❑ Perfection is essential. "I must be perfect to be successful" (You can double bogey in golf and still win the match.)

   ❑ Catastrophizing. "If I make one mistake, my partner (or parents or coach) will never forgive me." (Will they really hold it against you forever?)

   ❑ Worth = achievement. "If I don't do this right, I'm worthless." (My worth doesn't come only from this task.)

   ❑ Blaming. "The umpire favored the other team." (I can't control the officiating, but I can control my performance.)

   ❑ Dichotomous thinking. "I have to be the star pitcher on the team or I won't play." (I don't have to be the star to play on the team and contribute and enjoy the game.)

   ❑ One-trial generalization. "I can't play well in the rain because the last time I played in the rain, I played poorly." (Even though I didn't play well the last time I played in the rain, I do play well in any weather.)

6. Construct affirmative statements. Use your lists of what you like about yourself, what makes you unique, and what your successes are (chapter 2) to construct positive, action-oriented self-statements affirming your competence to be what you want to be, to do what you want to do, and to be as happy as you want. Aren't you glad you made the lists? Examples

of an affirmative statement are, "I play golf well in the rain," "I concentrate easily," and " I am enthusiastic." "Hit it firm" and "Roll it to the center of the cup" are also positive statements (see the appendix for more detailed information on constructing affirmative statements).

For the next two or three rounds of golf, listen to what you say to yourself. When you identify a negative thought, write it down and use the guidelines to convert the negative thought to a positive thought. Before you know it, you will be playing better golf.

INTEGRATION EXERCISES—GETTING YOUR MIND AND BODY TO WORK AS A UNIT

> "Concentration is a fine antidote to anxiety. I have always felt that the sheer intensity Ben Hogan applied to the shotmaking specifics was one of his greatest assets. It left no room in his mind for negative thoughts. The busier you can keep yourself with the particulars of shot assessment and execution, the less chance your mind has to dwell on the emotions"if" and "but" factors that breed anxiety."
>
> — *Jack Nicklaus*
> Professional Golfer

Exercises to improve fundamentals

Timing. Get a piece of string or some dental floss and tie a washer or bolt on the end of it. Swing the washer back and forth and notice how smoothly it moves. Observe how much time it takes for the washer to swing in one direction, pause, and then move in the other direction.

Now try to get it to move faster. Did the smooth flow of activity stop? Did the washer move less distance?

Weight drill. Take your 3 wood and some lead tape to the driving range. Don't be afraid to take my book along, too. Looking at a book on the driving range is apt to get a few chuckles and there's nothing like a little laughter to relax you. Here's what you do.

1. Take your 3 wood and apply some lead tape behind or on top of the club-

head. Increase the swing weight of the club by about three or four swing-weights (D3 or D4 for men and D0 or D1 for women).

2. Without using a golf ball, pick a spot of grass over which to let your golf club travel. Address this area.

3. Take a nice, slow, easy swing back and stop at the top.

   ❑ Were you able to feel the club activate parts of your hands and arms?

   ❑ Did you notice anything about your grip? Try it again, paying attention to your grip.

   ❑ Did you have to grip the club more tightly?

   ❑ Were you able to feel your backswing?

   ❑ Did the clubhead feel heavier at the top?

4. Take your backswing another half-dozen times and see how it feels. Become aware of how it feels and memorize those feelings.

5. Once you have completed the backswing drill, take a full swing using the grass as the area over which you want your club to travel. How did it feel?

   ❑ Was your pace faster or slower?

   ❑ Did you feel your body react to the club?

   ❑ Did the slower pace help you to make a weight shift?

   ❑ Did you feel that the club was giving you kinesthetic cues* that helped your pace?

6. Now tee up a ball and take a full swing using this new pace.

   ❑ Did your swing feel the same as when you did not have a ball in front of you?

   ❑ How was the ball flight?

---

* Kinesthetic cues are signals given by the position of your body so that other parts of your body react the way they should. For instance, if you were falling over, the position of your body would send a signal to your brain, which would extend your arm or move your leg to help you maintain your position. Of course, this happens in a milli-second, much too fast for you to decide what you are going to do. The golf swing will work in much the same way if you let your body give kinesthetic cues that will cause other parts of your body to react correctly. If you are not aware of how kinesthetic cues contribute to learning physical skills, you may want to read the section "Learning Methods" found in the appendix.

❑ Did it differ from the usual with the increased swing weight of the 3 wood?

❑ Was the trajectory the same or different?

7. Hit another dozen balls and see if there is an improvement in your timing.

8. Did the weight change your pace? If it did, than you have benefited from the drill.

9. If you found this drill helpful, include it in your practice routine perhaps once every four times you practice.

Exercises to improve thought control

1. Identify your thought patterns. During a practice round of golf, identify and write down any thought you have about your ability to make a golf shot or that predicts the outcome of the shot. You may also want to mark down the result of your golf shot. After the round, sit down and mark a minus sign in front of each statement you considered negative and a plus sign in front of each statement you believed was positive. Count the positive statements and negative statements. This should tell you whether you need to work on thought control.

2. Validity of statements. With the list of thoughts that you made in drill #1, challenge the validity of each negative statement. Note into which irrational thinking pattern each statement falls. Most of us have one dominant flaw in our thinking pattern. This drill should help you correct yours.

3. Using thought control. Use the guidelines for thought control in the Skull Practice for every negative thought you have on the course. Do this until you can break your negative thinking pattern.

SECTION C

STEPPING UP FROM THE BASICS: IMPROVING YOUR GOLF FUNDAMENTALS

> "Being a left-handed golfer is a big advantage. No one knows enough about your swing to mess you up with advice."
>
> *— Bob Charles*
> Professional Golfer

If you patiently read through the first four chapters, digested the material, and completed the exercises, you are on your way to playing better golf. In sections A and B I tried to help you to become an "active" golfer. By making the transition to the role of an active golfer, you became aware of your lifestyle and how you approach the tasks in your daily life, a round of golf, the course, the hole, and each golf shot. You probably found out that the way you approach each of these tasks is similar to the way you approach life in general. If you are methodical on the practice range, you probably found out that you are methodical on the course. A fly-by-the-seat-of-your-pants person approaches golf by the fly-by-the-seat-of-your-pants method. This is not to say that the "flyer" is not able to become a better golfer; it will just take a little more work.

This new awareness may have temporarily interfered with your flow and even your score. I like to look at it as a short-term inconvenience for a permanent improvement.

In section C I will discuss golf fundamentals and how they apply to lowering your score. Chapter 5 will address putting; chapter 6, chipping; chapter 7, pitching; chapter 8, the full swing. Why do I discuss putting first and the full swing last? Because you have to learn how to walk before you learn how to run. It is easier to learn the mental skills on simple strokes than on a more complex swing.

The SKULL PRACTICE: LEARNING THE MENTAL SKILLS section at the end of each chapter contains exercises designed to help you to achieve muscular relaxation, which, in turn, will help you to achieve mental relaxation. Learning the mental skills may be accomplished on a different schedule from your reading. I recommend that you read one chapter at a time, taking a week to practice the mechanical and mental skills.

CHAPTER 5:

PUTTING: THE MOST IMPORTANT

STROKE IN THE GAME

Passing through Rome in 1961, Sam Sneed stopped for an audience with Pope John. The golfer had not been playing well for some time, and he confessed to one of the papal officials: "I brought along my putter, on the chance that the pope might bless it." The monsignor nodded sympathetically. "I know, Mr. Sneed," he said. "My putting is absolutely hopeless too." Sneed looked at him in amazement. "If you live here and can't putt," he exclaimed, "what chance is there for me?"*

A PGA teaching pro told me that his putting was falling apart. He was concerned about this because he was preparing for the mini-tour. He thought perhaps it was a mental problem. After talking, we agreed to play a round of golf and exchange some information. He would teach me some course strategy and I would help him with his putting.

On the day we played golf, I assumed his fundamentals were correct and asked him about his putting. I wanted to learn about his thinking patterns. His approach to putting and his thought patterns seemed fine. He believed he could putt better: his lag putts could be closer and he thought he should make most putts that were within his ability. On the first hole he told me he was mentally reviewing his

* *Anecdotes*, Fadman, Little, Brown and Company, Boston.

81

putting fundamentals, and within a couple of holes he began to roll in some pretty challenging putts.

In the past, his routine address position for putting was with slightly opened shoulders. He had unknowingly moved away from that position over time, and that was the cause of his putting problems. Later he told me that after reviewing his fundamentals, he perceived that he was holding his shoulders square to the line of target. He changed his alignment by opening his shoulders slightly. He said that this better allowed him to see the line of his putt.

How did I help him? Although the factor interfering with his putting was not a typical mental error such as stress, lack of visualization, negative thoughts, or lack of confidence, I helped him reduce his anxiety about looking for an answer to his putting difficulty. The factor interfering with his putting was a simple alignment problem. Could he have found the interference without my help? Sure he could. Did I help? Yes. I made it easier for him to evaluate his fundamentals without any accompanying anxiety and provided an atmosphere for him to open his mind for change.

You can learn several lessons from my experience. The first is that golf is a dynamic game. Without realizing it we are constantly changing the way we set up to the ball, the way we hold the club, and the way we swing. It is easy to slip into habits that promote difficulties instead of peak performance. This easily occurs with alignment, weight distribution, initiating our backswing, initiating our forward swing, and visualizing the path or flight of the golf ball. You can reduce the chances of developing bad habits if you follow a set routine. I feel so strongly about having a pre-shot routine that I devoted an entire chapter to it. The more aware you are of your routine, the greater the chances that you will maintain it. Your pre-shot routine will help you to become consistent, and consistency helps you to maintain good habits.

The second lesson is that a problem with your game may not be mental even when you think it is. If you are not sure whether the problem is with golf fundamentals or mental skills, I suggest that you look into your fundamentals (grip, posture, and stance) first and make sure that everything is exactly as you want it. If your fundamentals are not satisfactory, consider taking a lesson or two to get them back in shape. If your fundamentals are acceptable, then you will have to evaluate your mental processes. Later in the book I'll teach you how to do that.

We can also learn that even a golf professional, trained in the fundamentals of the game and trained to teach others how to play golf, can gradually get off track. If this happens to a trained professional, what can we expect of ourselves? We can expect to make mistakes and develop some bad habits. No one is perfect. All we can do is attempt to make the fewest mistakes possible by developing a routine for assessing the hole, creating the shot, and maintaining a positive mental attitude. Then we need to carry out our plan every time we play golf.

In this example, the PGA pro needed feedback about his putting. That enabled him to assess what he was doing and correct the problem. The average golfer is usually not trained sufficiently for self-assessment. As he or she approaches a single-digit handicap, self-assessment becomes more possible. But it helps to know that even professional touring players have a teaching pro with whom they work. Most of us need to go to someone with a trained eye to help us with our fundamentals.

If it had turned out that my playing partner had sound fundamentals, I would have pursued a more vigorous evaluation of his mental skills. For the average player to be successful at playing golf and to lower his or her handicap, several changes must occur. The golfer must understand the fundamentals of the golf swing, must know what can interfere with the golf swing, must know what *is* interfering with the golf swing, and must know how to eliminate that interference. My goal for this chapter is to help you understand some of the fundamentals of putting that lend themselves to mental intervention, identify what can sabotage these fundamentals, and generate some solutions to deal with these barriers.

THE GOAL OF PUTTING

When you think about putting, what touring pros come to mind? Nicklaus? Lopez? Trevino? Norman? Carner? While most of us will think about our favorite touring professional as the best putter, the statistics for the putting leaders* list players who are not necessarily in the news. What stroke average would you consider acceptable? Is an average of 2.0 acceptable? Do touring pros have as their putting goal an average of 1.0? Perhaps a 1.5!

Some putting leaders on tour include senior tour members Lee Trevino, with 1.704, and Don January, with 1.613 (Vantage Cup statistics). PGA members George Burns (1.753), Payne Stewart (1.745), Greg Norman (1.752), and Paul Azinger (1.753) were ranked in the top ten through August 1990 (Nabisco Tour statistics).

What is our mission when we are on the green? Hitting the ball into the hole? Rolling the ball to the center of the cup? Which do you think gives you the best concept of putting? Hitting or rolling?

When I think of "hitting" something, I think of force. We hit a nail with a hammer and force it into a piece of wood. Whenever we think of hitting the ball into the hole, we think in terms of force. Synonyms for the word "hit" are smack, swat, punch, sock, slap, and whack. I would not want to think about the result of my putting stroke as "smacking the ball," "swatting the ball," or "whacking the ball." I don't think that force is the mindset we want for putting. In fact, in my opinion a mindset of force anywhere in the golf game is detrimental. I prefer to think of my putting stroke as "rolling" the ball.

When I think of rolling the ball to the center of the cup, I think of a smooth,

---

* Putting leaders are listed as the average number of putts per green reached in regulation.

delicate, easy movement. The mindset of smooth, delicate, and easy is compatible with the movement you make when you stroke the putter. It's a slow, smooth, easy, delicate movement.

The putting stroke is the simplest of the golf movements. It is a one-lever stroke with a pendulum-like movement. Your goal is to roll the ball to the center of the cup. To achieve this, you want to minimize extraneous movement and maximize essential movement. To minimize extraneous movement during the putting stroke you need to keep most of your body as quiet as possible. The putting stroke uses only your upper body; more specifically, only your arms and shoulders. Everything else stays quiet. To accomplish this quietness, you will see golfers go into all sorts of contortions— pointing their knees in, taking a really wide stance, or locking their wrists in position. How much of this contortion is necessary is a point of debate.

Second, you want to maximize the essential movements in your putting stroke. The essential movements are those of the large muscles of your arms and shoulders. By using the large muscles, you can gain consistency and accuracy because you are minimizing the variations in your setup and stroke. By varying the length of your backstroke while stroking the putter at a consistent speed, you are more accurate than if you moved the putter back the same distance each time and varied the speed of the forward stroke.

THE FUNDAMENTALS OF PUTTING

During the 1990 Senior Skins Game, Bryant Gumbel of NBC Sports Television asked Jack Nicklaus this question: "What goes through your mind when you putt?" Nicklaus replied,

> "The process. I line it up. Look at what I think I want
> to do. Get it in my mind positively how I want to hit
> it. Then, I get there, line it up, and do it. When I'm
> ready . . . maybe five seconds, maybe thirty seconds
> [I'll putt]."

Within this quote are many of the essential elements of putting, both mechanical and mental. Can you recognize those essential elements? Before you read on, read Nicklaus' quote again and underline each key word. Then list these words below.

1. _____

2. _____

3. _____

4. _____

5. _____

6. _____

Here is the quote again with the key words italicized. Nicklaus replied:

> "The *process*. I *line* it up. *Look* at what I think I want
> to do. Get it *in my mind positively* how I want to hit
> it. Then, *I get there, line it up* and *do it*. When I'm
> *ready* . . . maybe 5 seconds, maybe 30 seconds [I'll
> putt]."

When Nicklaus says that the "process" goes through his mind, what does he mean? The process he is talking about is lining up the putt, visualizing how the ball will roll, programming the stroke, and positively setting in his mind his stroke and the picture of the ball going into the hole. When he is ready, he addresses the ball and putts.

Notice that the process of putting doesn't include thinking about how many strokes ahead or behind he may be, the double boggy he may have made one or two holes back, or the birdie on the hole before that. He is not thinking of how much money he will win if he sinks this putt or what trophy he will take home. He also doesn't say that he is thinking of his grip or his stance or that he wants to keep his head still.

You can focus your attention on the process of golfing *or* on the outcome of the match that you are playing. One will enhance your performance, the other will hinder it. What do I mean by outcome thinking? You know. How much you will win if you sink this putt. What your partner will think if you miss. How good a putter everyone will say you are if you sink it. How you think about coming up short every time you have a long, uphill putt like this. How poorly you play when the pressure is on. If I were playing in an important tournament, I might be tempted to think about the headlines in the sports page: "Fasciana wins the club championship."

A close cousin to outcome thinking is put-down thinking. Many golfers put themselves down and give away their self-esteem during a round of golf. The golfer who is putting uphill leaves it short, and exclaims "Hit it, Alice!" This implies that he is stroking the golf ball with less strength than is necessary, or "putting like a woman." A sexist remark? Sure! It is also a remark that lowers self-esteem.

Another golfer may pull her tee shot and call herself a "dummy." Perhaps it was a bad shot, but that doesn't have anything to do with intelligence. We're all bound to make some stupid decisions on the golf course, as in life in general. Because we make a stupid decision doesn't mean that *we* are stupid.

Outcome thinking and put-down thinking hamper performance. Process thinking enhances it. What is process thinking and how do we do it? Process think-ing is paying attention to any part of the process of making a good golf swing or putting stroke. We could be thinking about swing cues, such as "slow" on the back-swing or "accelerate" on the forward swing. We might focus on the area over which we want our ball to travel. We could concentrate on the sound the club makes when it passes through the air. We could think of "set" on the backswing and "through" on the forward swing to help us with our timing.

Process thinking does not include thinking about instructions like Keep your head down, Squeeze tightly, or Keep your left arm stiff. Process thinking is target-related. Thinking about the target and where you want the ball to go is more produc-tive than thinking of mechanics. This is why process thinking enhances performance.

Let's take a look at the fundamentals of putting. Nicklaus mentioned the process, the target line, visualization, and execution. He did not address some of the other fundamentals, perhaps because they are so automatic for him that they are not in his conscious mind. The ones I describe here are the basics.

The grip

The connection between your body and your golf club is your grip. There are only a few basic rules about holding the putter. When you watch touring pros putt, you will see a large variety of grips, setups, and putters. One essential, however, is to grip the putter so that *its face is square to the target line*. This is absolutely neces-sary for consistent results. If your clubface is off slightly on your drive, it may mean 5 to 10 yards in the fairway—not very significant when you consider that the fair-way may be 70 yards wide. If your clubface is off on your approach shot to the green, it may mean 1 or 2 yards on the green—more significant, but not the end of the world. However, if your putterface is slightly off on a six-foot putt, the one or two inches that the ball goes left or right may well be the difference between making or missing your putt. Current thought on the hand position has the left hand turned counterclockwise "locking" up the wrist. The right hand "mirrors" the left hand.

> *Mental Approach*—Select a grip that is comfortable for you. This grip should *minimize any wrist movement*, since wrist putting tends to affect both direction and distance adversely. To maximize your feel, you need to hold the putter in your hands with light pressure. Tight grip pressure prevents you from feeling the putterhead. Ben Crenshaw suggests that your grip pressure should be light enough to allow someone to pull the club out of your hands.

The setup

Professionals use a variety of putting stances. Just remember that you must feel comfortable to be successful and you must be aligned to promote a pendulum-like stroke. The correct setup allows you to stroke the putter back and through without hampering your stroke. The basic setup is best described by the following:

❑ Align the putter

❑ Align your body at a right angle (square) to your intended target line.

❑ Distribute your weight evenly on both feet just behind the balls of your feet.

❑ Place the golf ball anywhere from inside your left heel to slightly ahead of the middle of your stance. If your stroke is more inside-square-inside than a straight back-and-forth stroke, where you place the ball in your stance is significant. It may mean several inches left or right on an 8-foot putt since the putter is square for only a couple of inches.

❑ Direct your eyes over the target line and behind the ball.

❑ Let your arms hang from your shoulders to promote a pendulum-like stroke.

Mental Approach—When you align your body, try to develop a pre-putt routine around the alignment of your putterface. This will allow you to setup your body in exactly the same way each time you are going to putt. With your body (feet, hips, shoulders, and eyes) square to the target line, you have the best chance to stroke the putter and roll the ball to the center of the cup. You can check your alignment on the practice green by using two 1" x 1" sticks. See the exercises at the end of this chapter.

Your weight distribution, ball placement, and eye placement will help you see your intended target line. If you are not comfortable, back off and start again.

The stroke

The putting stroke is a pendulum-like stroke made with the arms and shoulders. Only the arms and shoulders move; all other parts of your body remain still. This pendulum-like stroke goes straight back and straight through on the target line. The ball is struck during acceleration at the bottom of the forward stroke.

The ideal putting stroke is a backward movement followed by a slight pause followed by a forward movement. The backstroke is deliberate and uniform. The forward stroke is also deliberate and uniform and accelerates through the golf ball.

Mental Approach—The putting stroke errors I usually see are taking the putter back too far and then decelerating before impact and not taking the putter back far enough and then accelerating too fast. When you take the putter back too far, you subconsciously compensate by slowing down your forward stroke so you won't hit the ball off the green. When you don't take the putter back far enough, you subconsciously force the putter forward so that you won't be short.

To build consistency your putter should be taken back and forward at the same pace. Then in the forward stroke the putter will naturally accelerate through the ball before beginning to slow down. You may ask "How do I roll the ball different distances?" The answer is, by varying the distance of your backstroke. For example, let's say you can roll the ball eight feet using a one-foot backstroke and a one-foot follow through. If you want to roll the ball ten feet, you will want to take the putter back about fourteen inches. If you want to roll the ball four feet, take the putter back perhaps six or seven inches.

Natural pace and momentum and maintaining putter balance keep the face square. This process results in control.

The pre-putt routine

Several factors are important in developing a pre-putt routine.

    a. **Environmental assessment**—You need to evaluate the green. Are you putting uphill, downhill, or sidehill? Is the grass long or short? What kind of grass is it? Does it feel soft or firm under your feet? Did the ball check fast when you hit it to the green? Is it early in the day (grass may be short, greens may be moist) or late in the day (grass may be longer, greens may be drier especially if it has been windy)? What is the direction of the grain?

    Mental Approach—Once you have answered these questions, you need to put the data into your computer and adjust your stroke accordingly. Conditions that tend to slow your ball down will call for increased effort and consequently a longer backstroke and follow-through. Conditions that tend to speed up your ball will call for less effort and a shorter backstroke. For example, Bermuda grass has a heavy grain, which can alter the speed of your ball. Therefore you need to know which way the grass is growing. If the grass between you and the hole is dark, you are putting against the grain and will need a little more effort to get the ball to the center of the cup. If the grass is light, you are putting with the grain and will need a little less effort. With bent grass there is little grain, and you need to spend more time assessing the contour of the green. With rye grass, used as a seed-over grass in the winter, the ball should hold the line fairly well.

b. **Target**—The target in putting is the center of the cup. When stroking long putts, you may decide to lag the putt or putt to an area around the cup.

Mental Approach—Play the percentages. If, on fast greens, an attempt to roll the ball 20 feet to the hole could leave you with a treacherous downhill putt, you might want to avoid leaving the ball long and have a target six inches in front of the cup. Trying to leave it short without a specific target in mind will hamper your objective.

c. **Target line**—Although your target is the cup, you want to roll the ball along a line that will get the ball to the cup. Look for any imperfections on the green between you and the cup or any foreign objects on the green. If there are imperfections or debris, remove them before you putt, as the rules of golf allow.

Mental Approach—Decide on a target line only when you have attended to all the data and are sure that the line over which you want to roll the golf ball is the line the golf ball needs to take to roll into the cup. Your target line is related to the speed at which you will roll the golf ball.

Speed determines line. The faster you putt, the straighter the line will be—and the more difficult it will be to stop the ball at the cup. Determine the speed at which you will stroke the putter, then determine your line.

On long putts, your goal is to get the ball close. On short putts, your goal is to roll the ball to the center of the cup. Decide what you want to do with your putt, then do it. Trust your feelings. Don't second guess and don't look back.

d. **Visualization**—Visualizing your putting stroke will help you to consolidate in your mind the line that the ball will take to the target and the effort needed to get it there.

Mental Approach—Before you can putt consistently well, you must be able to "see" the ball go in the hole. Some people can visualize naturally, while others must learn how to do it. As a test of your imaging abilities . . . If I asked you to create an image of time flying what picture would come into your mind? Close your eyes now and create an image of time flying. Was your image that of the world spinning like a top? A plane flying through time zones? A rocket with a clock chained on top of it? An alarm clock with wings? Let's go with the alarm clock with wings. Close your eyes again and imagine in your mind's eye an alarm clock with wings . . .

Did the alarm clock have a bell on top of it? One or two bells? What color was the clock? What color were the wings? What time was on the clock? Well, maybe that last question was too much, but I think you get the idea. Whenever you are going to putt, you can increase your chances of getting it close, if not in the hole, by visualizing the stroke you are going to make and the way the ball will roll to the cup. When you visualize your putt, be sure to "watch" the ball drop into the cup.

e. **Programming stroke**—Using all the information that you have gathered up to this time—the distance to the cup, the slope of the green, the grass, and the target line—you can determine what effort you must make to roll the ball to the center of the cup. Once you have decided on your effort, you need to simulate your putting stroke.

Mental Approach—Nicklaus' statement that he would "set what I want to do in my mind positively" is related to this step. First he would set what he wants to do: roll the ball into the center of the cup. A picture, so to speak, of his proposed putt. Second, he would create the feel for the effort needed to roll the ball exactly the way he saw it in his mind. Both are essential if you want to increase your success rate on the greens.

Using the target line over which you have decided to roll your golf ball and the effort that you need to accomplish your objective, you now need to program the stroke you are going to make. Make this stroke a few times. (If you prefer to do your programming stroke at the address position rather than here, go to the next step.

f. **Pick an intermediate target**—This is the time to decide whether you want to pick an intermediate target. Intermediate targets are very useful when you cannot see your actual target, such as when you are attempting a 35-foot putt. They are less useful in short putts.

Arguments for picking an intermediate target are: 1) an intermediate target will show you a spot over which you want the ball to roll, 2) an intermediate target will take your mind off the mechanics of the putting stroke and put your mind on a target, and 3) having an intermediate target will diffuse tension about making the putt.

The argument against an intermediate target is that it will take your attention away from exactly where you want the ball to go—in the cup—hindering you from being able to stroke the ball the correct distance.

Mental Approach—Nicklaus uses an intermediate target when he putts. I believe this method increases your chances of meeting your goal.

g. **Practice stroke**—A practice stroke will help you to consolidate your programmed stroke and your visualization of how you want the ball to roll. If you decided that you want to take your programming stroke at the address position, this is the time to do it. Take your practice stroke and "watch" the ball roll to the center of the cup.

Mental Approach—The most important advice I can give to you is probably this: continue to take a practice stroke (with visualization) until you are convinced it is the stroke that will roll the ball to the center of the cup. If you are not sure, you are not ready to putt.

h. **Aim**—However you want to aim the putter face down the target line is acceptable within the rules of golf.

Mental Approach—Once you have aimed the putter face, build your stance around it. Building your stance around your putter promotes proper alignment. The opposite approach, aiming your body first and then adjusting your grip, is less effective. You may turn and twist to align yourself, and when you stroke the golf ball, you will inadvertently untwist and send the ball toward an unintended target.

i. **Get comfortable**—You must feel comfortable to be relaxed.

Mental Approach—You must feel comfortable and able to make a stroke that will take the putter back and through without altering the squareness of the putter. If you don't feel comfortable, start again.

Execution
Once you are comfortable, stroke the ball and roll it to the center of the cup.

Debriefing
Depending on the success of your golf shot, you should take a debriefing stroke. The purpose of this step is to mentally reinforce a stroke with which you are happy or to reprogram the correct stroke after you have made a mechanical error.

Postscript

You can do a couple of good deeds for the game of golf. First, you will make the game more pleasant for golfers following you if you fix your ball marks (and other people's). A ball mark that is fixed when it is made will fill in within 24 hours. If it is not fixed, it can take as long as three weeks to repair itself completely.

Second, you can protect the cut of the cup. Have you ever stroked a golf ball with a firm stroke to see it hit the back of the cup and fall into the hole? A great feeling, isn't it! The golf ball fell in the hole because the cut was square, not beveled. Golfers who have never been taught how to protect the cut of the cup may carelessly press the pin against the dirt or use their putters to retrieve their ball from the cup. These things bevel the cut of the cup, preventing the next golfer from experiencing the joy of watching his or her ball hit the back of the cup and fall in.

SKULL PRACTICE: LEARNING THE MENTAL SKILLS—HOW TO BREATHE

> "It is not that you have to be better than anyone else, but you have to be better than you ever thought you could be. The disgrace is not in losing; it's in not trying. You should never be afraid to fail."
>
> —*Ken Venturi*
> Professional Golfer

Most golfers realize that stress and tension adversely affect performance. Stress creates physiological reactions that result in increased heart rate, blood pressure, perspiration, and respiration. Psychologically, stress affects the way you approach golf: you begin to make quick, nonproductive decisions. Your reaction time for fine motor coordination is reduced, you begin to worry about what may happen, you become anxious about whether you can perform, you become more rapidly fatigued, and your concentration deteriorates.

Tension tightens muscles and creates a greater tendency for brute force. This is O.K. if you are a weight lifter, but not if you are putting a sharp-breaking putt on a fast green. Muscle tension prevents the feel needed for most golf shots. Those that require fine motor coordination are especially vulnerable. Your putting and chipping strokes are most likely to deteriorate during times of tension.

Managing stress and tension becomes mandatory if you want to perform well. In the course of the next five chapters I will present a series of relaxation exercises designed to control stress and tension. If you do these exercises as I suggest, you will be able to attain a relaxed state before and during any competition. The exercises take only between 10-20 minutes, and will serve as building blocks for managing stress as well as for visualization. It is impossible for me to teach you how to visualize if you are not able to relax completely. The topic for this chapter is breathing.

Breathing is something we take for granted. While most of us breathe correctly, we can all learn something from some discussion. Learning how to breathe correctly is important because it is the easiest physiological system to control and can act as a cue to relax you during times of stress or tension.* There are three kinds of breathing: high, medium, and low.

❑ High (shallow) breathing results from lifting the shoulders or high part of the rib cage. This is a tension breath, allowing the least amount of oxygen into the lungs.

❑ Medium (intercostal) breathing is accomplished by the expansion of the chest. This is the most common breathing.

❑ Low (diaphragmatic) breathing is deep, allowing for the greatest amount of oxygen intake.

Deep breathing allows you to get the maximum amount of oxygen into your lungs to nourish cells throughout your entire body. Breathing can serve as a cue to relax you in any situation you perceive as tension-provoking. For example, if you answer the telephone a lot during the day, you might use the sound of the telephone to remind you to take a deep breath and hold it for a few seconds before answering the phone. This will relax you and give you the feeling that you are in control. Perhaps you look at your watch a lot. If you do, put a small dot on the center of the crystal; then each time you look at your watch, take a deep breath and relax. If you do a lot of driving, use each red light as a cue to take a deep breath and relax.

I would like you to practice taking a deep breath now. Fill your lungs as much as you can, including the upper parts under your shoulders. Continue to inhale, filling your stomach. Now just relax your chest and stomach and let the air out naturally, without forcing. Good. Repeat that three more times. Each time you let the air out, repeat the word "relax" in your mind.

Now let's practice total breathing. Inhale for a slow count of eight, hold your breath for a count of four, and relax and let the air out for a count of eight. Repeat this three times.

Practice breathing throughout the day. You may want to do the complete breath exercise twice a day, once as soon as you wake up and again at night as soon as you go to bed. Other good times to do the breathing exercise are just before

---

* I'll say more about the stress reaction and what can be done about it in chapter 11.

eating—it will tend to help you to relax and chew your food better, aiding diges-tion—when you get into the car before you go to work, at a stop light, before you begin a project, and so forth.

How can breathing help you on the golf course?
Whenever you feel tense on the golf course, take a deep breath and repeat the word relax as you exhale. You can do this before you start your pre-shot routine. During the next few chapters we will build on this basic skill to the point where you can relax your entire body and rid yourself of any tension in a matter of seconds just by taking a deep breath. Getting to this point takes time and effort. Not a lot of time and effort—but you need to do some work to get any benefit.

INTEGRATION EXERCISES—GETTING YOUR MIND AND BODY TO WORK AS A UNIT

Exercises to improve fundamentals
Grip pressure—The following exercises will help you to determine your optimum grip pressure.

a. Variable pressure exercise (without golf balls)—The objective of this ex-ercise is to determine your optimal grip pressure. Take your putter and as-sume your putting stance. With your eyes closed, take your putter back about one foot. Then stroke it with a one-foot follow through.

   Were you able to feel the putterhead stop and change direction? Let's do an experiment—hold your putter as tightly as you can and take a putting stroke. Were you able to feel the putterhead stop and change direction? Now hold your putter as lightly as you can without letting it fall and repeat the putting stroke. Did these two strokes feel different?

   Somewhere between these two extremes is your optimal putting grip pressure. Using your putting grip, hold the putter at a 45-degree angle to the ground. The pressure you need to hold the club at this angle is about the pressure you need to putt successfully. Now try your putting stroke. Repeat this exercise until you feel your arms connected to your putter head. Write down what you have learned.

b. Variable grip pressure (with golf balls)—The objective of this exercise is to confirm your optimal putting grip pressure. Take about a half-dozen golf balls and go to the practice green. Select a spot from which to putt. This spot should be flat, straight, and about six feet from the cup. Putt six balls using your tightest grip. Putt another six balls using your lightest grip. Then putt six balls using the grip pressure you discovered by holding the putter at a 45-degree angle to the ground. What did you learn from this experience? Write it down.

Setup—This exercise will help you to learn the correct setup and to have confidence that you are lined up correctly. You can learn body alignment in your own living room. You need a full-length mirror, a small cut-out paper plate to act as a target, and two yardsticks. Put the paper plate about seven feet from a wall. Place the mirror upright against the wall and then place a golf ball on the floor about three feet away from the mirror. The mirror should be to your right when you address the ball. Place one yardstick parallel and 3 inches outside your target line and address the ball. Place the other yardstick in front of your toes. Adjust the yardsticks so they are parallel. Address the golf ball again and look in the mirror to see if your body is aligned correctly. Your toes, knees, hips, shoulders, and eyes should be parallel to the target line. Practice this exercise until you are confident that you can set up correctly (see figure 1).

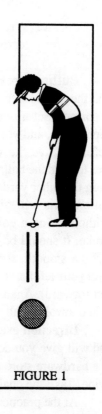

FIGURE 1

Eye alignment exercise—This exercise will show you where your eyes are when you putt. If you do not set up with your eyes at the same place each time, your golf balls may end up to the left or to the right. Your eyes must be over the line of the putt the way you would look down a rifle barrel aim. If your eyes are anywhere else, it would be like aiming your rifle while away from your body.

a. Preparation—Get a 10" x 10" mirror. Varnish a center spot about 2 inches square and add some sand before the varnish dries. The sand will give your golf ball a resting place. Tape two parallel lines (½" electrical tape is fine) equidistant from the varnished spot. These two lines should be about a putter-width apart (see figure 2).

b. Eye alignment exercise—Once the varnish has dried, do the following.

❑ Place the mirror on the floor or ground.

❑ Place a golf ball on the varnished area.

❑ Address the ball with your putter.

❑ Look in the mirror to see where your eyes are in relation to the ball.

❑ Practice putting with your eyes inside the target line, outside the target line, and behind the ball.

❑ Write down what you have learned.

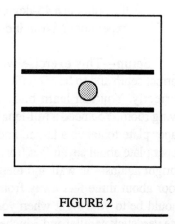

FIGURE 2

Putting stroke—This exercise will give you the confidence of knowing that your setup is correct. Set up your full-length mirror, your paper plate, and your two yardsticks as you did before. Move the yardstick that is near your toes toward the ball until it is only a little farther from the other yardstick than the width of your putter. This will give you a track along which to practice your putting stroke. Without using a golf ball, practice your stroke. At first focus only on your backstroke. It should be slow-paced and go straight. You may notice that it is easier to make a smooth, straight, evenly paced backstroke if you control the putter more with your left hand. Then practice only your follow-through (from the area of contact forward). Again, notice whether your stroke is more consistent if your left hand is in control. Finally, practice your entire stroke.

Direction exercise—This exercise will teach you to stroke the putter straight and will give you confidence that the ball will go in the direction you intended. Go to a hardware store and get a carpenter's blue chalk line, which is a ball of chalked twine. Take the chalk line, your putter, and six golf balls to the practice green.

At the practice green, select a hole with a flat, straight putt. Tie one end of the chalk line to the pin in the hole and hold the other end about four feet away from the cup. Snap the line against the green and a blue line will appear. Without using a golf ball, practice taking your putter back and through along the blue line. When you are satisfied with your stroke, putt a few dozen balls.

Distance exercise—This exercise will give you an idea of how far you putt a ball using various backstroke lengths while stroking the ball at the same pace. Take two yardsticks, a carpenter's line, your putter, and 10 golf balls to the practice green. Select a spot on the green that is straight and flat. At one end of the flat area place a tee in the green and mark off a ten-foot straight line with the carpenter's line. Make another parallel line about four inches away from the first line. Place a tee at each foot along the outside line and place the yardstick at the end of the line. You should have 11 tees, one at the beginning and one at each foot along the line. Place a golf ball at the 18" mark on the yardstick and do the following (see figure 3).

❑ Putt 10 balls taking the putter back 6 inches.

❑ Putt 10 balls taking the putter back 12 inches.

❏ Putt 10 balls taking the putter back 18 inches.

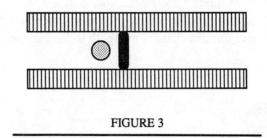

FIGURE 3

What have you learned from this exercise? Write it down.

Jeff Reich, head golf professional of the Karsten Golf Course in Tempe, Arizona, suggests you use one of the following three drills for distance:

❏ The lag drill—Take several balls to the center of the practice green and putt two balls to the fringe. See how close to the fringe you can get without touching it. Then aim in another direction at a different distance and lag to that fringe. Maximum putts in any one direction is two.

❏ Cluster drill—Take several balls and hit one in a specific direction. Without looking at the ball you just hit, strike another putt, attempting to duplicate the same feel. After hitting all the putts without looking up between strokes, check to see how "clustered" the balls are.

❏ One hand drill—Take a ball and hit it around the green with one hand only. Since you will not have much control of the putter, you will discover the importance of motion and pace in the stroke for solid contact.

Square contact exercise—This exercise is designed to help you to determine whether you are hitting the golf ball with the putterface square to your intended line. Take your carpenter's line, 10 range balls, and your putter to the practice green. Select a hole with a flat, straight putt and snap a line using your carpenter's blue chalk line. Place a range ball on the line with its stripe touching the line. The ball should be placed so that its line will roll over the blue line on the green. Putt a few dozen balls and watch the stripe. If you are hitting the ball on the sweet spot of your putter, with the putterface square, and in a straight line (pendulum motion), you should see the golf ball roll around its stripe until it stops.

Goalie exercise—This exercise will teach you how to roll the ball in a specific direction. Sometimes we get too target-oriented and have difficulty putting.

Select a flat spot on the practice green and place two parallel rows of tees on the green. The rows should be about 4 inches apart, and the tees should be spaced 6 to 8 inches from each other along their lines. Now putt a couple dozen golf balls through the channel. In this exercise you will be more interested in direction than in distance. You can also use this channel as a path to the cup (see figure 4).

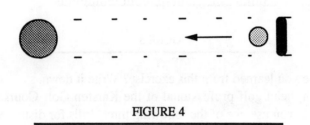

FIGURE 4

Confidence-building exercise—This exercise helps you create positive images of your success on the practice green. Take a chalk line, your putter, and a dozen golf balls to the practice green. Select a hole with a flat, straight putt. Mark a line 5 feet away from the cup and begin the following.

Putt 12 balls from 1 foot away. Focus your vision on the back of the cup and assertively drive the ball to that spot. This helps teach an authoritative stroke rather than "wishing" short putts in. Listen to the sound of the ball drop in the cup. Repeat this exercise from 1½ feet, then 2 feet, then 2½ feet, and so on up to 5 feet.

In doing this exercise, if you miss two or more from any one distance, drop back to the last distance and begin again.

Visualization—Take a chalk line, your putter, and a dozen golf balls to the practice green. Select a hole with a flat, straight putt. Mark a line 5 feet away from the cup. Place a golf ball on the line about 4 feet away from the cup. Without your putter, make a motion with your right hand as if you were pushing the ball toward the hole. After you make this motion, "watch" the ball roll to the center of the cup. Do this several times. Now with your putter, take a practice stroke and "watch" the ball roll to the center of the cup. When you are convinced that your practice stroke is the one needed to roll the ball to the center of the cup, putt the golf ball.

If you are having a difficult time with this you may want to learn how to visualize in reverse. Select a spot that gives you a straight putt about 4 feet from the cup. Place the ball on the green. Set up to the ball and putt the ball into the hole. Without moving, close your eyes and "watch" the replay of this very putt. Watch it several times until you see the action of the ball rolling into the hole. Memorize this picture so that you can recall it later when you are playing. Now take the same putt and putt it again. This time, go through your pre-putt routine and visualize the ball going into the hole. Set up to the ball and putt it. Try the same routine for some breaking putts, some that break to the right and some that break to the left. Do this for about an hour.

Warmup exercise—Select an area on the green and, with several tees, mark a target area 20 to 25 feet away. Practice rolling balls to within a foot of this area. Next, move in to about 15 feet and repeat the exercise. Now move in to about 10 feet. After warming up your stroke, select a hole and practice putts from 5 feet to one foot.

Exercises to improve breathing

The purpose for correct breathing is to increase awareness while reducing stress and tension, resulting in better feel and control.

Learning the whole breath—Sit or lie down in a comfortable position. Loosen clothing around your neck and chest. Take a deep breath and fill your lungs completely. Be sure your stomach and upper lungs fill with air; you will know you are doing this part correctly when your shoulders rise automatically. Take a few seconds to experience how an expanded chest feels, then let the air out by simply relaxing the muscles holding the air inside your lungs. Repeat this 8 or 10 times. Do this exercise at least a dozen times a day for three days.

Connecting the whole breath with relaxation—Repeat the whole breath exercise. Take a few seconds to experience how an expanded chest feels, then let the air out by relaxing the muscles holding the air inside your lungs. When you let go of your muscles say the word "relax" to yourself. Become aware of how the muscles feel when they are relaxed. This is the feeling you want to achieve in a state of relaxation. Repeat this exercise about a dozen times a day from day four through day six.

CHAPTER 6:

CHIPPING: GETTING INSIDE THE

LEATHER

"As the saying goes, 'nothing in life worthwhile comes easy'—this is especially true in sports. Without dedication, perseverance, courage and pain, there are no winners. To me, a winner is an individual who sets out to accomplish something and in the end, win or lose, can say to himself, 'I gave it my best'."

— *Jim Mueller*
Sportscaster

My wife and I are weekend golfers. Arriving at the golf course as a twosome, we are sometimes paired with another couple, but more often than not we end up with two men. We always get a chuckle out of the expressions of some of the men as we approach the first tee and they realize they are paired with a woman. You can almost hear them thinking, "Oh no, a woman, what a way to ruin a Saturday morning." Yes, there are still these types around, even in the 1990's!

When we are paired with sexist types, we always know we are in for some fun. Jane hits her tee shot 150 to 160 yards, almost always down the middle of the fairway. It takes perhaps three or four holes before we get any feedback that the men we are playing with have backed away from their original assumptions about playing with a woman. In about another three or four holes, this type generally begins to get irritated: Jane is outscoring them.

In spite of her shorter drives, Jane is a successful golfer because she plays within herself and because her short game is very good. Although it may take her three shots to reach the green on long par 4's, her shot to the green is usually in one-putt range. Jane's specialty is the chip shot.

Let's do some imagery. Vividly imagine yourself in the following situation. You are on the #1 handicap hole at a new course (par 4, 390 yards). The hole is a slight dogleg left. The fairway is narrow and flat and lined with trees on both sides. You hit your tee shot 235 yards in the middle of the fairway. Your approach shot is correct but ends up 5 feet from the left margin of the two-tiered green. You are about 40 feet from the cup, which is placed on the lower tier. The green slopes gradually from left to right. You realize that if you land your ball on the lower tier, you will roll the ball well past the cup. Your shot is to chip the ball to the upper tier and let it break and roll down the tier to the cup. The break you read is about 10 feet; your proposed landing area is on the green about 10 feet to the left of the cup.

How are you feeling so far? Anxious? Worried about getting close enough to one-putt? You don't have to feel anxious or worried if you have a good chip shot in your golf bag.

Few golf shots have greater potential as confidence builders than the chip shot. Consistently getting the ball to the hole in tap-in range is always a terrific boost to your morale. It also demoralizes your opponents.

THE GOAL OF CHIPPING

The goal of the chip shot is to get the golf ball inside the leather, reducing your putt to a "give-me." In planning your chip shot you can intend to roll the ball to the center of the cup, but don't be discouraged if it doesn't make it, leaving you with a 1 to 1½-foot putt. If you can chip within this range, you have been successful.

THE FUNDAMENTALS OF CHIPPING

The chip shot is used when you are very close to the fringe of the green and cannot use a putter. This distance is generally several feet but can be as much as 15 feet. It is really an extended putt using a lofted club to get over an obstacle. There are two reasons for choosing to chip rather than putt from the fringe. The distance between you and the green is too great to predict accurately the effort needed to get the ball close to the cup, and the terrain between you and the green is not uniform and so is unpredictable.

The most popular method of chipping is to use a lofted club with a full-swing grip. The club is stroked somewhat like a putter*: a single-lever stroke without breaking your wrists as described in the last chapter.

A variation in the chip stroke is the grip pressure you use. I would pass on this

---

* The difference with chipping is that your hands, at address, are set much ahead of the ball—at about the crease on the pants of your left leg. The relative relationship of your hands to the ball remains the same throughout the stroke.

grip pressure variable unless you are a scratch golfer with an outstanding ability to use grip pressure. Since this golf shot is so important, if you have not had a lesson on the chip shot, I suggest you do. After a lesson you can practice the variables so that you can become an expert chipper.

The following are the basic principles of chipping.

Club selection

In chipping the most important principle is the use of *minimum air time and maximum ground time.* With this in mind, you will want to select a club that will get the ball on the green as soon as possible, then have it roll to the cup. You will need some basic information about how the golf ball reacts using different clubs and how much carry and roll you get using the same club while varying the backstroke and follow-through. Employing the same stroke with the most lofted club can send the ball higher for a shorter distance in the air with less roll. Employing a less lofted club can send the ball lower for a longer distance in the air with more roll.

> *Mental Approach*—If you have been using the same club and varying the speed of your swing for chipping, you may want to do the exercise at the end of this chapter that demonstrates the reaction of the golf ball when different clubs are used with the same basic stroke.

The grip

The grip used for the chip shot is the full-swing grip.

> *Mental Approach*—Whichever grip you choose, you can increase the variety of possible shots using the same stroke and the same club by varying your backstroke length. You will need to experiment with different clubs and different lengths of backstroke.

The setup

The setup for the chip shot is as follows.

    a. Body alignment—Align your body slightly to fairly opened.

    b. Weight—Your weight is distributed slightly forward with 60-70% of your weight on your left foot.

    c. Ball—Your ball is placed from the back-of-center of your stance to even with your right foot.

    d. Hands—Hands are ahead of the ball at the crease of your left pant leg.

    e. Eyes—Eyes are inside the target line and in front of the ball.

The stroke
Your chip shot should stay in the air a minimum length of time and roll on the green a maximum length of time. That is to say, you should attempt to have the ball land on the green as soon as possible and allow it to "run" all the way to the center of the cup. During the stroke your weight stays on your left side. The club is taken back and then through. Your legs stay quiet. This is more an accuracy shot than a distance shot. Most professionals try to keep the chip shot consistent by using the same stroke every time they chip. They change the club to make the golf ball roll different distances.

> *Mental Approach*—Don't confuse "the same stroke" with the same length of backstroke. The "same stroke" means the same pace or the same effort. The amount of backstroke means how far back you take the golf club. No matter what the amount of backstroke, your effort should be the same. Increased clubhead speed is generated by taking the club back farther, with greater acceleration caused by the greater distance the club travels, not by the force of your hands or arms.
>
> You should spend some practice time grooving your stroke so that the only variables are that of your club and your backstroke.

The pre-chip routine

a. Environmental assessment—From behind the ball, evaluate the following. Is your landing area flat? Uphill? Downhill? Sidehill? In what direction will the ball go when it hits the green? Is the grass long or short? What kind of grass is it? Does it feel soft or firm under your feet? How high is the grass at the spot where the ball is lying? Where is the grain of the grass there? What kind of stance do you have for this shot?

> *Mental Approach*—Having evaluated, you have an idea of your choices.

b. Target—The target in chipping is the spot from which the ball will roll to the center of the cup.

> *Mental Approach*—You have evaluated the green conditions and selected a target. With this information, you are able to select the loft of the club and the effort (amount of backstroke) needed to roll the ball to the center of the cup. Note: Given the same set of circumstances, the target for your shot will change depending on these two variables.

c. Target line—Evaluate the green in determining your target line. You will want to remove any debris and fix any imperfections between you and the cup, as the rules of golf allow.

Mental Approach—It only takes a few seconds to clean up the green, so don't have the attitude that debris doesn't matter. Not following through on this easy task could produce some disappointing results.

d. Visualization—Visualizing how your ball will fly to the green and how it will roll to the hole will help you to create the shot you need either to sink the ball or get it to one-putt range. Because more things can happen to the golf ball with chipping than with any other golf shot, you must be able to recall what happens when you hit the golf ball with each club. Visualization involves integrating what is required to make the golf shot with what you know you can do with a specific golf club.

Mental Approach—When you visualize your chip shot, you want to be able to "see" your ball go into the air, land and roll to the cup. Your visualization will differ depending on which club you select. If you want your ball to go high and stop fast, visualize how this will occur. If you want your ball to fly low and roll far, visualize this action. Be sure to "watch" the ball drop into the cup.

e. Club selection: Why, you may ask do I have "club selection" after visualization? You would think the thing to do would be to select the club before you visualize the shot you are going to hit. While this is true in most other golf shots, in chipping it is more productive to do it the other way around. First plan the shot you want to execute, then select the club that will generate that shot.

Mental Approach—To be a successful chipper you must have a clear picture of how you want the ball to fly as well as a picture of how each golf club will propel the golf ball. Then it becomes a matter of matching the club with the task at hand.

f. Programming stroke—Using your intended target line, program the stroke you are going to make. Integrate your programming stroke with the picture of the ball landing in the target area. Be sure to continue your visualization and "watch" the ball go into the hole.

Mental Approach—You know how you want the ball to get to the cup. You have selected the club that will create the shot that you have in

105

mind—more lofted for high shots that stop rapidly and less lofted for low shots that roll a lot. You now want to program the stroke that will create your golf shot. Take your selected club and address an area close to the ball, without risking an accidental hit. Stroke the club exactly as you plan to hit the ball. Then "watch" the ball fly in the air and roll to the cup. With experience, you will know whether you have selected the correct club and the correct amount of effort. If you are not sure whether your selected club will produce your visualized shot, you can do one of two things: spend more time on the practice green until you are able to recognize the golf shot created by each club, or perform a mental trial-and-error sequence until you are confident of your club selection and your intended shot. Obviously, the time to learn club selection and performance of the club is not while you are playing but on the practice green.

g. Pick an intermediate target—You may not need an intermediate target if you can see your actual target. If you cannot see the target, you should pick out an intermediate one.

Mental Approach—You should always have either an actual or an intermediate target in performing a chip shot. It is the only way for you to integrate your club selection, your effort, and your intended golf shot. Otherwise, hitting the golf ball is like shooting craps.

h. Practice stroke—A practice stroke is as important on a chip shot as it is on a putt. If you are able to visualize your chip shot, the ball in flight, and the roll to the pin, you can actually sink a respectable number of chip shots. I keep "practicing" my stroke until I'm sure that what I feel is the stroke that will send the ball to the cup.

Mental Approach—You know how you want the ball to fly, how you want it to roll, and what club to use, and you have programmed your stroke. Now you need to practice the actual shot you are going to make. I would practice the shot perhaps 2 to 5 times until I was sure I had it right. In reality you will probably take the same number of practice strokes each time you make a chip shot. This will become a part of your pre-chip routine.

i. Aim—Aim is very important in chipping, because if you are not holding the clubface square to the landing area, you can push or pull the ball. You can also compound your error by putting left or right spin on the ball, which will cause it to go more left or right than you expected. If you are not sure of your ability to aim the club properly, a chipping lesson and practice will do wonders for your game. It is helpful to have a ball with lines, like a range ball, to see how the ball spins when you hit it. If you don't have any range balls, use a magic marker to paint lines on your practice balls. Once you have aimed your clubface, build your stance around it.

Mental Approach—You need to develop a method of lining up your golf club with your intended target line. The factors you should pay attention to are the squareness of the club face, your body alignment, and the plane in which you are going to move the club. The most recommended way to aim is to line up your club face first, then build your stance around the club face.

j. Get comfortable—As in any golf shot, you must feel comfortable when you address the ball. You mus also be in a position to see your target and able to make a stroke that will take the club back and through without altering the squareness of the golf club.

Mental Approach—In working with mini-tour golf professionals, I am often struck by the observation that when they made a poor golf shot they were not comfortable. Perhaps they were standing too close *to* the tee marker, or they were not lined up exactly the way they wanted, or one of their feet was in a depression on the tee. My advice is that whenever you are uncomfortable, back off and begin again. I don't swing my club until I am sure I have selected the correct club, picked out an intermediate target, programmed either a timing or actual swing, and that I am comfortable in the address position.

Execution
Once you are comfortable, strike the ball and send it to the hole.

Mental Approach—If you have done everything correctly to this point, all you need to do is let it happen.

Debriefing
Depending on the success of your golf shot, you should take a debriefing swing. The purpose of this step is to reinforce mentally a swing you are happy with or reprogram the correct swing after you have made a mechanical error.

To illustrate the mental aspects of chipping, I have included five examples.

1. You are chipping from the edge of the green (2 feet) to a relatively flat

green, with the pin placed 15 feet from the edge of the green. What do you want the ball to do? What club would you select?

2. You are chipping from the edge of the green (2 feet) to a green that slopes uphill away from you with the pin placed 15 feet from the edge of the green. What do you want the ball to do? What club would you select? Are there other factors to consider? If the grain is against you, how will this affect your decision? Are there any circumstances in which you would want to hit the ball harder?

3. You are chipping from the edge of the green (5 feet) to a moderately upsloping green with a pin placement 35 feet from the edge of the green. What do you want the ball to do? What club will you select?

4. You are 10 feet away from the fringe of the green and the pin is 15 feet away from the edge of the green. The green slopes away from you downhill. How do you want the ball to travel? What club will you select?

5. You are 10 feet away from the edge of the green and the pin is placed 15 feet away from the edge of the green. You elect to chip with an 8 iron. Your partner's ball is 2 feet to your right. He chooses a 9 iron for his chip shot. Will you both land the ball in the same area?

Comments on the examples:

1. You probably want the ball to land on the green as soon as possible and roll to the center of the cup. In a flat green, it won't take much effort to roll the ball 15 feet from where it lands. Therefore you would probably select a sand wedge or a pitching wedge and an appropriate backswing to accomplish this task.

2. You want the ball to land quickly on the green and roll to the center of the cup. To accomplish this, you may have to consider some additional factors. How much does the green slope? If this is Bermuda grass (has grain), are you hitting into the grain or with the grain? In all likelihood the grain is against you, because grass usually grows in the direction of drainage and water.

   If you think you have to hit the ball harder, select a different club. Remember, you want the club to do the work. All you want to do is to take your basic chipping stroke and select the club that will get the job done with that stroke. If, when you take your programming stroke, you feel you have to hit the ball harder given the club you have selected, you need to change clubs. If you change clubs and are still not sure, evaluate all the factors again and select the club that is suitable. I can remember times when I changed clubs three times, to the irritation of my playing partners, and holed the chip.

3. You want the ball to land on the green as soon as possible and roll to the center of the cup. Thirty-five feet is a long distance to chip a ball. In this case you may elect to use the 7 iron with a backswing of about 2½ feet.

4. You want the ball to go high and stop rapidly. You would probably select a sand wedge.

5. Probably not.

SKULL PRACTICE: LEARNING THE MENTAL SKILLS—HOW TO RELAX YOUR BODY—PART 1

In the last chapter, I discussed how learning to manage stress and tension could effectively prevent performance deterioration. I taught you how to breathe deeply to create a relaxed state.

In this chapter I will teach you how to relax your muscles. First, however, you need to know the difference between tense muscles and relaxed muscles. Edmund Jacobson, MD, has a technique for relaxation that he developed in his medical practice. Jacobson noticed he had many patients who complained of various symptoms but who did not respond well to the medications prescribed for them. These patients appeared tense; they frowned and wrinkled their foreheads. Was stress at the root of their symptoms?

Jacobson guessed that it was. Believing that "an anxious mind cannot exist in a relaxed body," he showed his patients how to relax their bodies, on the assumption that their minds would respond in kind. The series of exercises he taught required the contraction of one set of muscles followed by the relaxation of the same muscles. The exercises progressed throughout the body from one set of muscles to another, first tensing, then relaxing. Jacobson called this "Progressive Relaxation."

As Jacobson learned from his patients, there are both physiological and psychological benefits to be gained from the Progressive Relaxation exercise. Learned relaxation of skeletal muscles can help relax smooth muscles in the blood vessels and digestive system, resulting in lower blood pressure and a slower heart rate. Progressive Relaxation can also help relieve tension headaches. Psychological benefits include an improvement in self-concept, a reduction in depression and anxiety, relief from insomnia, and a more positive mental attitude over time, Jacobson's patients had fewer complaints related to stress and tension.

About the relaxation-visualization exercises

There are five relaxation-visualization exercises that are necessary for you to learn to control stress, to release tension, to visualize your golf shot, and to visualize your performance. The first exercise is *Progressive Relaxation* (Part 1) that follows this discussion. PR teaches you how to relax your muscles by contrasting tension and relaxation. The second exercise, *Progressive Relaxation* (Part 2) is contained in chapter 7 and teaches you how to relax your muscles without first tension them. The third exercise is *Autogenic Training* which teaches you to create sensations in your body. Autogenic Training is found in chapter 8 and is a vital link between relaxation and visualization. The fourth exercise, *Visualization*, is found in chapter 9. It teaches you skills to visualize your golf shot. The last exercise, *Previewing Performance*, will teach you how to see yourself performing well. This exercise is found in chapter 10.

Each exercise must be mastered before going on to the next if you want to receive the most benefit. You need to tape record the text of each exercise and listen to it at least once a day for about 7-10 days. Once you have mastered the exercise, you can do it without the tape. If you do not want to record your own voice you may have a friend record the text for you. If you wish to purchase a pre-recorded tape of exercises, there is an order blank at the end of the book.

An acceptable plan to learn the exercises is as follows:

      a. Practice *Progressive Relaxation*—Part 1 (chapter 6) once a day for a week.

      b. Practice *Progressive Relaxation*—Part 2 (chapter 7) for one week.

      c. Practice *Autogenic Training* (chapter 8) for one week.

      d. Practice *Visualization* (chapter 9) for one week.

      e. Practice *Previewing Performance* (chapter 10) for one week.

Preparation for Progressive Relaxation

❑ Select a quiet room.

❑ Dim the lights.

❑ Remove or loosen any tight clothing.

❑ Remove contact lenses.

❑ Be sure that the room is warm.

❑ Remove your shoes.

❑ Select a comfortable chair or lie on the bed.

❑ You may place a pillow under your knees and neck.

❑ If you have arthritis or dental appliances, you may wish to skip the tension part and just do the relaxation part.

When recording the text, pause about 10 seconds after each contraction so that relaxation can occur completely, and pause about 15 to 20 seconds each time you see three asterisks (***) in the text. *You should follow these instructions for every relaxation exercise appearing at the end of chapters 6,7,8,9, and 10.*

READ THESE INSTRUCTIONS
INTO YOUR TAPE RECORDER

1. Sit or lie down in a comfortable position.

2. Close your eyes and take a slow, deep breath. Inhale as much air as you can.

3. Exhale slowly and completely, allowing the tension to leave your body. Just let the air come out by itself. ***

4. Begin by making a fist with your dominant hand. Squeeze hard and feel the tension. *** Feel the tension and relax. ***
    Notice the difference between tension and relaxation. ***
    Make a fist again and feel the tension, ***
    and relax without putting any effort into relaxing. ***

5. With your other hand, make a fist. Squeeze hard and feel the tension, ***
    and relax. Notice the difference between tension and relaxation. ***
    Make a fist again and feel the tension, *** and relax. ***

6. Now clench both fists. *** Feel the tension and relax.
    Let all the muscles in your arms become relaxed and loose.
    Clench both fists again, *** and relax. ***

7. Bend your elbows and tense your biceps, *** and relax.

111

Let your arms gently fall back into a comfortable position.
Bend your arms again, *** feel the tension and relax.
Allow yourself to experience how good it feels to be relaxed.

8. Now straighten out your arms in front of you and tense your triceps.
    Tense them hard, *** and then relax. Just let the relaxation happen. ***
    Again, tense your triceps, *** and relax.
    Let the tension leave your body. Let your body relax more and more. ***
    As you relax more and more, you may feel sensations of warmth or
    heaviness, or you may feel so light that you feel you can float away.
    Let the feelings happen and relax deeper and deeper. ***

9. Focus on your facial muscles.
    Raise your eyebrows and wrinkle your forehead, *** and relax. ***
    Tense your eyebrows and forehead again, *** and relax. ***
    Feel the tension leaving your forehead and your eyes. ***

10. Now frown and squint your eyes, *** and relax. ***
    Tense your eyes and brows again, *** and relax. ***
    Feel the relaxation moving over your face and scalp like a wave.
    Notice how good that feels. *** Keep your eyes gently closed.

11. Clench your teeth together, feel the tension in your jaws, *** and relax.
    Repeat the tension in your jaws, *** and relax.
    Notice the difference in sensations when your jaw is relaxed.
    Do you hold tension in your jaws?

12. Push your tongue against the roof of your mouth, press hard. ***
    Then relax. ***

13. Press your lips together as tightly as you can, *** and relax.
    Whenever you let go of tension, you can get more deeply relaxed. ***
    Notice how relaxed your arms and your head are.
    Notice how good that feels. ***

14. Now shrug your shoulders up.
    Feel the tension in your shoulders, neck, and upper back, *** and
    relax.
    Bring your shoulders forward and feel the tension, *** and relax again.
    Notice how your neck and upper back relax.
    Notice how relaxed the different parts of your body are.
    hands, *** arms, *** eyes, *** cheeks, *** jaws, *** lips, ***
    tongue and throat.

15. Take a deep breath. Fill the lower part of your lungs, the middle part, and the upper part and notice the tension. ***
    Now relax. Notice how the air just drains out of your lungs.
    Continue to breath normally and relax. ***
    Notice how each time you breath out you relax deeper and deeper.
    With each exhalation, relax more deeply (*pause* for 30 seconds).

16. Now take a deep breath and fill your lungs completely. ***
    Let the air drain from your lungs.
    When all the air is out of your lungs, push as much out as you can and stop breathing. Notice how uncomfortable the tension feels.
    Now breathe normally again. ***

17. Tighten your stomach muscles as if you were about to get hit
    in the stomach. *** Feel the tension, *** and relax.
    This time push your stomach out as far as you can, *** and relax.
    Notice how the wave of relaxation spreads throughout your stomach, chest and upper back. ***

18. Tense your buttocks and thighs by pressing your heels against the ground as hard as you can. ***
    Notice the tension, *** and relax. ***

19. Now curl your toes and notice the tension, *** and relax. ***
    Notice how the wave of relaxation travels through your legs and feet. ***

20. Now just relax for a couple more minutes. ***
    Let the wave of relaxation travel throughout your body. ***

21. Let's do a slow body scan. ***
    Pay attention to your head.
    Notice how relaxed your scalp and forehead are. ***
    Notice how relaxed your facial muscles and your eyes are. ***
    Feel the relaxation in your lips, tongue, and jaws. ***
    Notice how this wave of relaxation spreads into your neck and throat. ***
    Feel your shoulder muscles relaxed and your arms and hands relaxed. ***
    Your back and chest feel completely relaxed. ***
    Observe how relaxed your stomach is. ***
    Notice how relaxed your hips and thighs are. ***
    Follow this relaxation into your legs and feet. ***
    Notice how great it feels to be completely relaxed and free of tension. ***

Notice the feeling of warmth.

22. Memorize these feelings of freedom, relaxation, and goodness, knowing that you can learn to achieve these feelings any time you want to.
    (*Pause* for 30 seconds).

23. Count backward from 5 to 1. During that time you can wake yourself up, and when you wake up you will feel relaxed and refreshed, alert and alive and good in every way. 5 *** 4 *** 3 *** 2 *** 1.

INTEGRATION EXERCISES—GETTING YOUR MIND AND BODY TO WORK AS A UNIT

Exercises to improve fundamentals
Club-ball flight relationship. As with any other golf shot, you must learn the mechanics thoroughly and know what you want to accomplish before you strike the golf ball. Once you know how to hit a chip shot, you need to practice. You will need to learn how the golf ball reacts using the same stroke but different clubs. A simple exercise will teach you this. Take a couple dozen "retired" balls and paint a line around each of them so that they look like range balls. Take your sand wedge, pitching wedge, 9 iron, 8 iron, and 7 iron to the practice green. Pick a spot from which to hit. The hitting area should be flat, with a flat target area. Without using any golf balls, practice your basic chipping stroke. Take the club back about 2 feet, then forward, following through about 2 feet. Practice the basic stroke twenty or thirty times. Now, using the basic chipping stroke you just practiced, take a sand wedge and hit a dozen balls at about a one-foot distance from the edge of the green.

What happened when you did this exercise? The ball should have gone high, landed close to you and rolled very little. Most of the golf balls should have gone about the same distance. Now use your pitching wedge and repeat this exercise. Notice what happens. Repeat using your 9 iron, then your 8 iron, and then your 7 iron. You should have gained four pieces of information: the ball flight pattern, the distance the ball travels, the amount of roll that you get from each club, and how the golf ball spins when you strike it and how this spin affects the direction of the ball when it lands on the green. Now you know what to expect from each club (did you use the same stroke even though you changed clubs?) and will be able to select a club for any situation. Eventually, when you have learned the feel of each club and what happens to the golf ball, you can move on to greater things and learn what happens when the green slopes away from you, what happens when the green slopes toward you, and what happens when the green slopes left or right.

Grip pressure. Once you have learned about club selection and ball flight, you can experiment with grip pressure. Select a flat part of the practice green and a

9 iron. Hit a half-dozen balls with your normal grip pressure. After you see where the balls come to rest, hit another half-dozen balls using a slightly firmer grip pressure. If you have done everything the same in the two sets, those balls that you hit with a firmer grip should be a foot or so farther than those that you hit with your regular grip.

Exercises to improve relaxation

Awareness of tension exercise. Sit or lie down in a comfortable position. Pay attention to the various areas of your body. Start with your head and work your way through your face, shoulders, back muscles, stomach muscles, legs, and arms. As you travel through your body, see if those areas are tense or relaxed. Don't try to do anything, just identify whether they are tense or relaxed.

    Body scan. Repeat exercise #1. This time, whenever you find an area that is tense, release that tension. You can connect the release of tension from those muscles to the exhalation phase of your breathing cycle. When you find tension, exhale that tension while breathing by repeating the word "relax." This is an important exercise to practice, because before swinging the golf club or putting, you may want to do a quick body scan. Remember, most of us hold tension in our neck and shoulders.

CHAPTER 7:

PITCHING: THE BRIDGE BETWEEN

THE FAIRWAY AND THE CUP

> A pessimist is one who makes difficulties of his op-
> portunities; an optimist is one who makes oppor-
> tunities of his difficulties.
>
> — *Harry Truman*

My uncle Joe is the master of the "bump and run." He can hit a golf ball from 50 to 60 yards out and put it within one-putt range 85 percent of the time. Uncle Joe is a very successful golfer on his home course of Fox Hill Country Club in West Pittston, Pennsylvania. When I first learned to play golf he would tell me that I needed to learn this golf shot. Of course, I was stubborn and wanted to see the high pretty shots landing softly on the green. I was not as successful with my "pretty" shots as he was with his "bump and run" shots, but I believed that one should learn to use all the clubs in one's bag. Just between you and me, Uncle Joe was successful on his home course because the greens at Fox Hill are at the same level as the fairway, with no front sand bunkers to foul up his kind of shot. When he went to play on other courses, he couldn't use his favorite shot. If you believe, as I do, that you need to learn how to use all the clubs in your bag, this may be an interesting chapter for you.

As you did the chipping exercises in the last chapter, you probably observed that, as you got farther away from your target, it became more difficult to reconcile the pace of your basic single-lever chipping stroke with your objective of getting the ball to the target. As you moved farther back from the green, you may have felt that you either had to swing harder or break your wrists to generate enough clubhead speed to get the ball to the green. Swinging harder would only have sabotaged your timing. Breaking your wrists might have allowed you to accomplish your goal—

117

getting the golf ball to the target—but you would probably have resisted this since you were practicing chipping, a one-lever stroke. You can stop worrying about all this now, because in this chapter I am going to discuss the pitch shot, and you can go out in the back yard or to the golf course and break your wrists to your heart's content.

THE GOAL OF THE PITCH SHOT

The goal of the pitch shot is to get the ball safely over any hazard or over a specific area of the fairway and land it on the green. Ideally, you will land your golf ball on the green within one- putt range.

THE FUNDAMENTALS OF THE PITCH SHOT

The pitch shot is used for a high (lob) shot to the green with the purpose of stopping the ball quickly. It can be used anywhere from a few feet off the edge of the green to as much as 75 yards out. The pitch shot has less chance of going into the hole since it is less accurate than the chip shot, which is less accurate than the putter. (Greg Norman may disagree with this statement if he remembers Robert Gamez's pitch shot to win the Nestle Invitational Tournament, Bay Hill Club and Lodge, Orlando, Florida.)

ACCURACY: *MOST* ————————————> *LEAST*

PUTT —> CHIP SHOT —> PITCH SHOT

However, although less accurate than the chip shot, the pitch shot offers the greatest variety of golf shots. You can use your creativity in pitching a golf ball to the green by selecting a different club, a different length of backswing, or both. Selecting a different club alters the ball flight and its action on the green. Varying the length of your backswing alters the speed of the club at impact, assuming you swing it at the same pace. This variety of clubhead speed at impact would subsequently vary the distance that the golf ball travels. Using the same swing, you can create a golf shot for a variety of situations.

The following are the basic principles of pitching.

Club selection

The rule of minimum air time and maximum ground time applies less to pitching than it did to chipping, depending on your style of play. If your style is to send the golf ball past the hole and back it up, maximum air time and minimum ground time applies. If, on the other hand, your style is to pitch the ball to the green and let it roll, you may prefer less air time and more ground time.

Depending on your style, if you have enough green to work with (15 to 20 yards out), you may elect to use a club with less loft to allow the golf ball to roll after landing on the green. If you are pitching over a bunker and the pin is cut close to you, you might select a more lofted club in order to carry the bunker and stop the golf ball quickly.

Mental Approach—If you have the ability to back up the ball when pitching to the green, you may want to learn both styles of pitching. However, you can be very successful with the style of pitching to the green and allowing the ball to roll.

The grip

The grip used for the pitch shot is the normal, full-swing grip. Where you grip the club will vary according to the distance you intend to hit the ball.

Mental Approach—If you wish to take some distance off your pitch shot, one way to accomplish this is to choke-down on the club. In doing so you essentially make your swing plane more upright and shorten your arc. Shortening your arc will reduce clubhead speed. The result of choking down is a higher shot, less distance, and less roll. You will want to experiment on the practice green to get a feel for what I am describing here.

Another important point in the grip is to maintain a light grip pressure. Remember, the pitch shot is still a finesse shot. It almost requires that you have a soft feel to your arms and hands. If you are holding the club too tightly, you may hit the golf ball too far or allow the ball to run too much. The ideal feel for the pitch shot is soft arms.

The setup

The setup for the pitch shot is as follows:

a. Weight. Evenly distributed.

b. Ball. Placed in center to slightly ahead of center.

c. Hands. Ahead of the ball.

d. Eyes. Inside the target line and over or slightly behind the ball.

The swing

The swing used for the pitch shot is a "partial" full-swing shot. I use the word "partial" because the pitch shot is not a full golf swing. It is a golf shot in which the degree of your backswing, given a specific club and swing effort, determines the distance the ball travels. Golfers usually consider three backswing positions with respect to the position of their arms: the nine o'clock position, the 10 o'clock position, and the 11 o'clock position. Using the same swing pace, each of these positions will propel the ball specific distances. The nine o'clock position is used for a shorter distance than the 10 o'clock position, which is used for a shorter distance than the 11 o'clock position. Most golf professionals keep their swing effort the same, varying only the club and their backswing position. This is the simplest way to handle the great variety of golf shots and their results. It is probably the best way to maintain consistency in your short game. If you were to combine these three backswing positions with a variety of golf clubs, say, the 7 iron, the 8 iron, the 9 iron, the pitching wedge, and the sand wedge, you would have enough options to create the exact golf shot needed for almost any situation.

> *Mental Approach*—The most important aspect of the pitch shot is probably the rhythm of the swing. If you want to be consistent, you'll need to develop and maintain the same pace, speed, effort, and finish. Only the club selection and the backswing distance should change.

The pre-pitch routine

a. Environmental assessment. From behind the ball, evaluate the following. Is your landing area flat? Uphill? Downhill? Sidehill? In what direction will the ball go when it hits the green? Is the grass on the green long or short? What type of grass is it? How high is the grass where the ball is lying? Is the grain with or against you? What kind of stance do you have for this shot?

> *Mental Approach*—The environmental assessment is as important in pitching as it is in chipping or putting. These factors will influence your choice of clubs as well as your choice of effort on your backswing. The grass on which your ball is lying is a particularly important factor. If the golf ball is fluffed up by tall grass, it will go higher and shorter and will roll farther—no backspin—since grass is caught between the ball and the club. If the grain of the grass is against you, you may have to play the ball slightly back to prevent the grass from slowing the club down before you hit the ball.

b. Target. The target in pitching is generally the area near the pin. The more lofted your club, the closer your target will be to the pin. Thus, choice of club helps determine choice of target.

> *Mental Approach*—Depending on your skill level, you may want to have

as your target: anywhere on the green, the quarter of the green where the pin is placed, or the pin itself.

c.   Target line. Evaluate the green before determining your target line. If the green is tiered, you may decide to pitch the ball closer to the area where the pin is cut by using a more lofted club.

Mental Approach—Depending on what is between you and the green, you can generate options for your ideal target line. Sometimes you can save a stroke or two by having the green opposite where the pin is placed as your target.

d.   Visualization. Visualizing your pitching swing will help you to create the shot you need to get it within one-putt range. When you visualize your pitch, be sure to "watch" the ball hit the green and roll to the pin.

Mental Approach—When you visualize your pitch shot, you want to be able to "see" your ball go into the air and land on the green. Your visualization will differ depending on which club you select. Your visualizing skills will improve with practice. When you have had enough experience seeing how the ball goes with each club, you will be able to recall the image of the golf shot and visualize how the ball will go.

e.   Programming swing. Using the target line you decided on for your pitch shot, program the swing you are going to make with the picture of the ball landing at the target. A programming swing is important because of the variety of clubs and variety of backswing lengths that can be used. Each created swing will have its own unique pattern of how the golf ball will fly, land, and roll. Be sure to complete your visualization and "watch" the ball come to rest.

Mental Approach—One way to learn whether your programming swing was correct is to become aware of the difference between it and your actual swing. If your actual swing is faster or if you swing harder, either you selected a club that was too lofted or you selected too short a backswing. If your actual swing is slower or you decelerate going into the ball, either your club was not lofted enough or your backswing was too long.

f.   Pick an intermediate target. Because, in most pitch shots, you are too far from your target to aim for it, you need to pick an intermediate target to help you to aim the club along your intended target line.

Mental Approach—You should always have an intermediate target in executing a pitch shot. It is the only way to integrate your club selection, your effort, and your intended golf shot.

g.   Practice swing. A practice swing is essential for a pitch shot to integrate your programming stroke with your visualized shot. Before I hit a pitch shot, I keep practicing the shot until I'm sure that what I feel is the swing that will get the golf ball where I want it to go.

Mental Approach—Once you have decided which club and which backswing you are going to use, you need to practice the swing with the club and get a feel for what you believe the ball will do once you strike it. Take as many practice swings as you need. Don't hesitate to select a different club. Often you will see a golfer take a practice swing. He or she will decide to take a different club, take several other practice swings, and then hit a poor shot. It may seem that whenever a golfer takes a different club, he or she does not make a good shot. I contend that the second club still didn't feel right and the golfer went ahead with it anyway.

h.   Aim. Aiming the club for the pitch shot is the same as aiming for the full shot. From the eight o'clock position, aim the clubface down the target line and at the intermediate target. Position your feet perpendicular to the target line, grip the club, and reposition your body. If you like, you may open your stance for the pitch shot.

Mental Approach—If you have not developed a method of lining up your golf club with your intended target line, you should develop one soon. Pay attention to the squareness of the club face, your body alignment, and the plane in which you are going to move the club. The most recommended way to aim is first to line up your club face, then build your stance around it.

i.   Get comfortable. As in any golf shot, you must feel comfortable and be in a position to see your target and able to make a swing that will take the club back and through.

Mental Approach—I suggest to golfers that they do whatever they need to do to become comfortable. When a golfer is uncomfortable, sometimes it is their club selection, sometimes it is the thoughts going through their minds, sometimes it is their setup. Whatever the reason, if they can isolate the source of their discomfort and overcome it, they will play better golf.

Comfort at the address position is very important. If you are uncomfortable, back off and begin again. Don't swing your club until you are sure you have selected the correct club, have picked out an intermediate target, have programmed either a timing or actual swing, and are comfortable at address.

Execution
Once you are comfortable, strike the ball and send it toward the hole.

Debriefing
Depending on the success of your golf shot, you should take a debriefing swing. Mentally reinforce a swing with which you are happy or reprogram the correct swing if you have made a mechanical error.

To illustrate the mental aspects of pitching, I have included several examples.

1. You have a golf shot to a green where the pin is cut 15 yards from the back. For the sake of argument, your choices for club selection are an 8 iron with a backswing to 9 o'clock, a 9 iron with a backswing to 10 o'clock, or a pitching wedge with a backswing to 11 o'clock. The 8 iron will travel lower and run a good distance on the green. The 9 iron will travel higher than the 8 iron and run less. The pitching wedge will travel the highest of the three and will run the least on the green. Which club would you choose?

2. If I changed the scenario and said that the green was two-tiered with the border of the tier running from 8 o'clock to 2 o'clock (viewed from your position), which club would you select this time?

3. Suppose I changed the scenario again and said that the green was severely upsloping?

The point to remember is that when selecting a club, you need to know how each propels the golf ball, you need to assess the particulars of your situation, and you need to have confidence in your selection—then swing to accomplish your goal.

Comments on the examples:

1. You might pick the one that gives you the most confidence and the most success. With a flat green you might pick the 9 iron with a 10 o'clock backswing.

2. With the border of the tier running angled to your ball path, you would want to avoid running the ball up the incline of the tier, since you would

have a difficult time predicting the exact break your ball would take. You would most likely decide to use a more lofted club to send the ball to the level of the green where the pin is cut and stop it quickly.

3. You might choose the 8 iron with a 9 o'clock backswing. Depending on the slope of the green, you might even decide to use the 8 iron with a 10 o'clock backswing.

SKULL PRACTICE: LEARNING THE MENTAL SKILLS—HOW TO RELAX YOUR MIND—PART 2

In the last chapter I discussed Progressive Relaxation, a method of tensing and relaxing your muscles to relieve stress and tension. I gave you an exercise that taught you how to tense your muscles to learn what tension felt like and how to relax your muscles to learn what tension-free muscles felt like. If you have done your exercises, you have probably become pretty good at relaxing. In this chapter I am going to go through the same exercise. This time I will ask you to relax your muscles without first tensing them. This exercise will teach you how to relax your muscles whenever you want to. As you progress in the relaxation exercises in this chapter and the next few chapters, you will learn to achieve faster and deeper relaxation—the key to mental control.

By this time you know the procedure for doing relaxation exercises, but I will repeat them again in this chapter. Please use these guidelines.

❑ Select a quiet room.

❑ Dim the lights.

❑ Remove or loosen amy tight clothing.

❑ Remove contact lenses.

❑ Be sure that the room is warm.

❑ Remove your shoes.

❑ Select a comfortable chair or lay on the bed.

❑ You may place a pillow under your knees and neck.

Again, read the directions into a tape recorder as you are doing the exercise for the first time, then listen to the tape when you practice the exercise later. Do this exercise only after you have mastered the exercise in chapter 6. Pause about 15 to 20 seconds each time you see three asterisks (***) in the text.

1. Sit or lie down in a comfortable position.

2. Close your eyes and take a slow, deep breath.
    Inhale as much air as you can.
    Exhale slowly and completely, allowing the tension to leave your body.
    Just let the air come out by itself. ***

3. Take another deep breath and let it out. ***

4. Take a few more breaths. Say the word "relax" while you exhale. ***

5. Focus on your dominant hand and allow it to relax. ***
    Release all the tension from your hand. ***
    Feel how good it is to relax your hand. ***
    Release the tension from you arm and relax it. ***

6. Now focus on the other hand and allow it to relax. ***
    Release all the tension from you hand. ***
    Feel how good it is to have your hands relaxed. ***
    Release the tension from your arm and relax it. ***

7. Focus on your facial muscles.
    Release any tension from your eyebrows and forehead. ***
    Feel the tension leaving your eyes and forehead. ***

8. Now pay attention to your scalp. ***
    Feel the wave of relaxation moving from your eyes and forehead to your scalp. ***
    Notice how good that feels. ***

9. Focus on your mouth.
    Relax your jaw. ***
    Release all tension from your jaw. ***
    Release all tension from your tongue. ***
    Release all tension from your lips. ***

10. Notice how relaxed your arms are. ***
    Notice how relaxed your head is. ***
    Notice how relaxed your mouth and jaw are. ***
    Enjoy the great feeling of being relaxed. ***

11. Pay attention to your shoulders. ***
    Release any tension from your shoulders. ***
    Feel the relaxation in your shoulders. ***

12. Let this relaxation move into your neck and upper back. ***
    Relax. ***

Relax your neck and upper back. ***
Notice how relaxed the different parts of your body are.
Hands *** arms *** eyes *** cheeks *** jaw *** lips *** tongue and throat.

13. Take a deep breath and allow these parts of your body to relax even more. ***
Continue to breath normally and relax. ***
Notice that each time you breath out you relax deeper and deeper. ***
Each time you breath, relax more deeply (*pause* for 30 seconds).

14. Release any tension from your stomach. ***
Your stomach sometimes holds tension during competition.
Release any tension from your stomach. ***

15. Let the relaxation go to your chest and lower back. ***
Notice how easy you are breathing. ***

16. Now relax your buttocks and thighs. ***
Let this wave of relaxation travel through your legs to your feet. ***
Feel how good it is when your legs and feet are relaxed. ***

17. Now just relax for a couple more minutes. ***
Let the wave of relaxation travel throughout your body. ***

18. Let's do a slow body scan. ***
Notice how relaxed your scalp and forehead are. ***
Notice how relaxed your facial muscles and your eyes are. ***
Feel the relaxation in your lips, tongue, and jaw. ***
Notice how this wave of relaxation spreads into your neck and throat. ***
Feel your shoulder muscles relaxed and your arms and hands relaxed. ***
Your arms and shoulders are relaxed and warm. ***
Your back and chest feel completely relaxed and warm. ***
Observe how relaxed your stomach is, *** how warm your stomach is. ***
Notice how relaxed your hips and thighs are. ***
Follow this relaxation into your legs and feet. ***
Notice how great it feels to be completely relaxed and free of tension. ***
Notice the feeling of warmth throughout your body. ***

19. Memorize these feelings of freedom, relaxation, and goodness knowing that you can learn to achieve these feelings any time you want to.
(*Pause* for 30 seconds).

20. Count backward from 5 to 1. During that time you can wake yourself up, and when you wake up you will feel relaxed and refreshed, alert and alive and good in every way. 5 *** 4 *** 3 *** 2 *** 1.

INTEGRATION EXERCISES—GETTING YOUR MIND AND BODY TO WORK AS A UNIT

Exercises to improve fundamentals

Learning the clock positions. There are two variables in the pitch shot: the club you select and the amount of backswing you take. As I stated before, the three backswing positions are the 9 o'clock, the 10 o'clock, and the 11 o'clock. The first lesson you should learn is the feel of each position. I recommend that you learn one position at a time—9 o'clock one day, 10 o'clock another day, and 11 o'clock the third day. If you decide that a shot to the green is a 9 o'clock pitching wedge, you need to have confidence that you can take your pitching wedge back to the 9 o'clock position and then execute the golf shot.

a. Learning the 9 o'clock position—To learn the feel for the different positions, take your 9 iron and a full-length mirror out to the back yard. Posi-

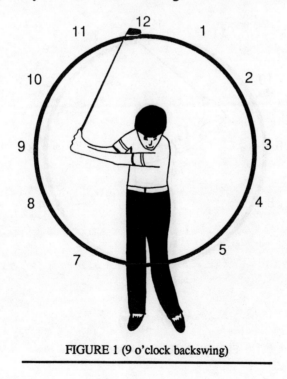

FIGURE 1 (9 o'clock backswing)

127

tion the mirror so that you can see yourself swinging the club. Set up for a pitch shot with your 9 iron. While looking in the mirror, move your arms to the 9 o'clock position and feel how your body is aligned. Without moving anything, look down at your arms to see how they look. Again without moving anything, look down at the ball and feel how your body is aligned. Repeat this exercise 15 to 20 times.

Next, address the ball. With your eye on the ball, move your arms to the 9 o'clock position. Try to determine, by feel, whether you really are in the 9 o'clock position. When you think you are, check yourself in the mirror. If you are not in the 9 o'clock position, start over from the beginning of this exercise until you learn to feel the 9 o'clock position. Do this 15 to 20 times.

b. Learning the 10 o'clock and 11 o'clock positions—Repeat the exercises just described with your arms at the 10 o'clock position. Repeat for the 11 o'clock position.

Putting the clock positions to work. Once you have learned the three clock positions, you will want to go to the practice pitching range. You must have the same feel for the different shots. Remember, you want to vary only the backswing

FIGURE 2 (10 o'clock backswing)

and the club, not the grip pressure or tension in your arms. Your arms should feel light and soft.

a. Pitching wedge at the 9 o'clock position—Pace off 30 yards from the pin and take your pitching wedge to experiment on distance. Hit about a dozen golf balls with your pitching wedge using the 9 o'clock position. If your golf balls are short or long, adjust your distance until you are hitting on the practice green. Pace this distance so that you have an accurate measurement of how far you hit a pitching wedge with the 9 o'clock position. Notice how the ball flies. Does it stop fast or does it roll? Mark the distance and how you felt in your diary.

b. Pitching wedge at the 10 o'clock position—From where you were hitting the balls in the 9 o'clock position, add 10 yards and hit a couple dozen balls to the pitching green. Adjust your distance accordingly and mark it in your diary.

c. Pitching wedge at the 11 o'clock position—From where you were hitting balls in the 10 o'clock position, add 15 yards and hit a dozen golf balls to the green. Adjust your distance accordingly and mark it in your diary. Note in your diary how the swing felt and how you felt.

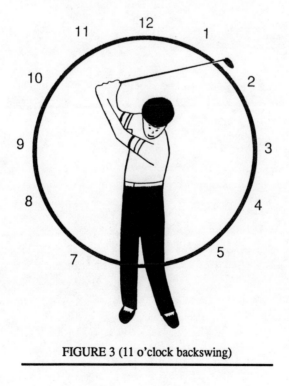

FIGURE 3 (11 o'clock backswing)

Learning the different clubs. Repeat the first two exercises using the 9 iron, then the 8 iron, then the 7 iron.

Exercises to improve relaxing your muscles

Body scan. Sit or lie down in a comfortable position. Pay attention to the various areas of your body. Start with your head and work your way through your face, shoulders, back muscles, stomach muscles, legs, and arms. As you travel through your body, notice whether those areas are tense or relaxed. Don't try to do anything; just identify whether they are tense or relaxed.

Body scan with release. Repeat the previous exercise. As you go through the various parts of your body, release any tension repeating the word "relax" while exhaling.

CHAPTER 8:

THE FULL SWING: FINALLY

"Harry, what is your handicap?" "My handicap? My
handicap is that Johnson is keeping score!"

"I have no trouble hitting the woods. My problem is
getting out of them."

"My favorite wood? My pencil."

"When I'm on a course and it starts to rain and lightn-
ing, I hold up my 1 iron, 'cause I know even God
can't hit a 1 iron."

— *Lee Trevino*
Professional golfer

The dream of many golfers is to live on a golf course. Their dream course is never
crowded; it never rains when you want to play; there are always very likable people
to play with; when you hit into the woods, the ball hits a tree and bounces to the
middle of the fairway; nobody ever talks while you are assessing your shot or are
ready to hit; nobody gives advice unless asked; and whenever you hit to the green
and miss, the ball bounces on the green toward the pin. On weekends, you can wake
up, get a glass of orange juice and a bowl of cereal, and walk out your back door to
the first tee. You can play a few holes after work or even before work. Maybe in
your dreams you don't have to work at all.

Well, so much for fantasy golf. I do live just a couple of blocks from a golf course, however, and living so close, I can practice very easily. I often visit the course in the late afternoon to practice some putting or chipping or whatever it is I am working on. Often I just sit and watch people on the driving range. If you've never gone people watching, I suggest you do. You will learn a lot about people and you'll learn a lot about yourself.

In watching people on the practice range you can easily tell the good players from the high-handicap ones. Good golfers look different—in the way they walk up to the ball, in how they address the ball, and in how they swing their golf clubs. High handicap golfers walk up to the ball without a plan, they look uncomfortable, and they swing fast—as if the ball is going to run off the tee if they don't hit it fast enough. Good golfers look as if they have a plan, they are never hurried, and they take their time swinging the club.

One day I arrived at the driving range and saw about a dozen young golfers hitting balls on the practice range. They all looked like they knew what they were doing. I got a bucket of balls and walked slowly over to the range. On the way I asked one of the golfers what was going on, and he replied that it was a tournament of the local teaching pros. I watched them swing for a while, and when most of them had finished, I started my practice routine. I had never hit as well as I did that day. I attributed my improvement to what I learned watching them practice. I suppose you could say that I copied their pace.

I don't think high handicap golfers understand the basics of the golf swing. Thinking of the swing as a wheel, I would say they are hub-oriented rather than rim-oriented. If you watch a wheel turn, you will see the hub, that is, the middle of the wheel, turning very rapidly in relation to the rim. The high handicapper swings as if he were playing the role of the hub—quick, compact movement, whereas the low handicapper swings as he were playing the role of the rim—slow, extended movement.

If high-handicap golfers understood their mission in striking a golf ball, they wouldn't swing at it the way they do. What they also don't understand is what they must do to strike the ball well. In this chapter I'll try to give you some insight into the golf swing and what happens when you swing your club.

THE GOAL OF THE FULL SWING

> "You don't hit anything with your backswing. So don't rush it."
>
> *— Doug Ford*
> Professional golfer

The goal of the full swing is to generate optimal clubhead speed at the moment of impact to propel the golf ball a desired distance in a specific direction.

THE FUNDAMENTALS OF THE FULL SWING

The golf swing is simply a sequence of movements backward (away from the target) followed by a sequence of movements forward (toward the target), resulting in the striking of the golf ball. That's all there is to the full swing. Of course the success of this motion depends on many factors, which I will discuss as we go along.

Following are the basic principles of the full swing.

Club selection

The club you select will usually be determined by how far you are from your intended landing area, how you would like the ball to get to this landing area (ball flight pattern), where the ball is sitting, where you are standing, and your level of skill. Regardless of what club you select, all of this assumes that you will hit a full shot. The movements are the same for all clubs. If there is any change in your setup or swing, it is the result of the length of the club and not the result of your conscious thought. Setup is the result of the length of the club, not the result of conscious thought.

Mental Approach—It helps to know how far you can propel a golf ball with each club. Of course, some days your ball will travel 5 yards more or 5 yards less, but, on average, you will drive it about the same distance. When you play golf, if you have not had time to loosen up on the practice range, you may want to take one club longer so you can set your pace to "easy" during the first two or three holes.

Another factor in club selection is determined by the location of hazards. If the trouble is mostly behind the green, play it safe and select a club that will get you to the front part of the green. If the trouble is in front of the green, take a club that will get you to the pin or to the back of the green.

Arnold Palmer, in his video on course strategy, suggests you play a round of golf using an iron one club longer than you would generally chose. He says you will be surprised to find that your score improves.

Do you have a golf club you can depend on even when the going gets tough? If you do, you may want to select a club for your drive or second shot that will leave you an opening for that club. I can depend on my 6 iron to hit a golf shot that will go a predictable distance in the correct direction. So on a par 5 I may use an iron instead of a wood on my second shot to put me into a position to use my 6 iron.

The grip

The legendary Ben Hogan describes the grip as "the heartbeat of the action of the golf swing." The grip is the connection between the power generated by your body and your golf club. It is the grip that allows the free flow of activity during the golf swing. It can transfer your energy to propel the golf ball, or it can obstruct the flow of motion. There are two important factors in the grip: where you place your hands and how tightly you hold the club. Let's talk about them.

a. Where you place your hands on the club. No matter what grip you select, your hands must be placed on the club so that they work as a unit. Each hand is placed so as to promote proper movement rather than restricting it and in a way that allows each to participate equally in the grip; neither hand dominates.

b. Grip pressure. When holding the golf club, you should feel the greatest pressure on the last three fingers of your left hand and the two middle fingers of your right hand. This pressure activates the inside muscles of your arms, which are responsible for a good swing.

Mental Approach—The best way to assure a solid grip is to put your hands on the club in the same sequence each time. This sequence should start with your aiming your golf club and then building your stance around that point.

The setup

Guidelines for the full swing.

❑ Weight—slightly on the right foot (60-70 percent).

❑ Ball—placed just inside your left heel.

❑ Hands and arms—in a straight line with the shaft of the club.

❑ Eyes—inside the target line and behind the ball.

Mental Approach—These are the basics of the basics. They promote a free flow of movements. If you set up correctly, you will be able to allow the simple swing I described earlier. Setting up correctly means positioning your body so you can swing freely and strike the golf ball in the direction of your target. If you don't set up correctly, you won't be able to execute an easy swing. During your sessions on the practice range, check these positions. You can use a mirror or a video tape. When you get in trouble, always go back to the basics: grip, stance, and alignment.

The swing

As I have said, the golf swing is simply a sequence of movements backward (away from the target) followed by a sequence of movements forward (toward the target), resulting in the striking of the golf ball.

Here is the swing in more detail.

The backward movement:

1. The golf club is swung back, away from the target with the hands, arms, and shoulders.

2. At some point in your swing you begin to move the club up and around your body so it is over your shoulders.

3. As your arms move the club in this arc, they pull your shoulders around.

4. Your shoulders, in turn, pull your hips around.

5. Your hips then pull your left knee and ankle to your right.

6. This movement of your left knee and ankle raises your left heel off the ground.

The forward movement:

1. Your left heel comes down and your knees move laterally (forward or toward the target).

2. Your legs lead the forward swing, pulling your hips toward your address position.

3. Your hips, in turn, pull your shoulders, which pull your arms.

4. Your arms pull your wrists and hands.

5. Your wrists and hands accelerate to catch up with your arms.

6. Your wrists and hands pass your arms and pull them up and around your body.

7. Your arms pull your shoulders in a forward arc.

8. Your shoulders pull your right hip and right leg.

9. Your right leg pulls your right heel off the ground.

Mental Approach—For the full swing, timing is everything. Why timing? Because you are moving a long club completely back and completely forward, and you are moving your body as well. We're talking about a long distance here. Remember I told you about the hub-directed golfers? They don't allow time for their swings to finish going back and then finish going forward. It is easy to spot them on the practice range or on the course. All you see is the blur of their arms and the club swinging around their shoulders. If you don't take the time to let the club go back all the way and then take your time letting the club pass through space to finish, you are rushing your shot, and the results are disastrous.

If you move your body too soon or too late, the ball cannot go where you want it to go. Too soon and you have a hook or a pull. Too late and you have a push or a fade.

The pre-shot routine.

a. Environmental assessment. From behind the ball, evaluate the following: Is your landing area flat? Will the golf ball tend to go left, right, or straight? How is your ball lying (if you are on the tee, this is less important). If on the fairway, is your ball sitting up on the grass? Is it buried in the rough? What about your stance—are you on solid footing? How are wind conditions? Is the flag moving? Are the tree tops moving? In what direction are they moving?

   Mental Approach—If you are on the tee, you have less to worry about, since you are able to select an area in which you can have a good stance and a good lie.

b. Target. Your target in the full swing is a landing area in the fairway or on the green. Your landing area in the fairway is a place from which you can hit the ball to the green. If your landing area is the green, it is to an area that lends itself to rolling the ball easily to the center of the cup.

   Mental Approach—You are concerned about your target area. Many golfers tee off without considering where, in the fairway, they want their ball to land. This is fine if you have a fairway as wide as a football field, but that is usually not the case. Another aspect of the target area, covered in the chapter on strategy, is where you would prefer to hit your next golf shot from. If the pin is on the right and protected by a sand bunker, you probably want to go in from the left, which means that your landing area is the left side of the fairway.

c. Target line. From the 7 o'clock position and with your ball flight pattern in mind, mentally draw a line from the ball to your intended landing area.

Mental Approach—You can visualize a target line as wide as you want. I usually see a 4-inch-wide channel along which I want my golf ball to travel.

d. Visualize the shot. After selecting a target line, visualize your ball traveling along that line and falling in your intended landing area. Watch the ball bounce and roll to a stop. Once you have previewed the flight of your golf shot, you may want to take a mini-swing to integrate the picture of the ball flight and the swing you must take to convert your visualized shot to reality.

Mental Approach—In visualizing your golf shot, complete your visualization. "See" the golf ball leave the club, fly through the air, land in the fairway or on the green, bounce once or twice, and come to rest. Once you "see" the ball come to rest, you have completed your visualization.

e. Programming swing. Unlike the putt, the chip, or the pitch, which require a partial stroke or a partial swing, when taking a full swing you don't need to take a programming swing to practice the effort needed to accomplish your goal. What you do need is a programming swing for timing. I like to think of this as a timing swing. Another way to look at a timing swing is as a mini-mini-swing.

Mental Approach—What you want to do is provide a signal for your body about what muscles will react and in what order they will react. The most simple and stress-free way of doing this is with a simple mini-swing. Take the club back and leisurely start your forward swing. Use a "cue" such as putting your left heel down, kicking off with your right instep, or a pull downward with your left forearm. Whatever works for you. Watch some of the pros on TV and you will see what I mean.

    You may want to attach a swing cue or a feeling to the swing to help you to execute your shot.

f. Pick an intermediate target. Approximately 3 to 8 feet in front of you, pick out a target in line with your ball and your intended target. This intermediate target will aid in your set-up and help guide your swing.

Mental Approach—On the tee, you have a great advantage in picking out an intermediate target. You can tee your ball behind a leaf, a brown spot in the grass, or anything you wish.

    Once you select an intermediate target, imagine a line connecting it and the golf ball. This imaginary line should extend backward a distance equal to the distance between the ball and your intermediate target. This helps in alignment.

g. Practice swing. A practice swing is not necessary for a full swing unless you are going to alter your normal swing.

Mental Approach—If you are intentionally going to draw or fade the ball, you may want to take a practice swing.

h. Aiming the clubface. From the 8 o'clock position, aim the clubface down the target line. Position your right foot perpendicular to the target line, position your left foot perpendicular to the target line, grip the club, and reposition your body. You may have a slightly different sequence of aiming the club. Once again, if you don't have a routine of aiming the clubface, you should develop one. As with any swing, your address position is built around the target line: first by aiming the clubface, then by aligning your body, then by gripping the golf club. Remember, you grip the club first, you may turn your hands to "square-up" the club; then, when you swing, your hands will return to the position you had before you turned your hands, and the clubface will no longer be square.

Mental Approach—How you aim your golf club will determine how you set up to the ball. How you set up to the ball will determine how you swing your golf club. If you are aimed incorrectly, you may block out either your back swing or your forward swing. Either of these situations will interfere with your objective of sending the golf ball down the fairway to your intended target.

i. Get comfortable. You must be comfortable to get your golf ball to where you want it to go. Do whatever you need to do to get comfortable. Most of the discomfort at this point arises from your being tense or rigid in your setup—grip, stance, or posture.

Mental Approach—Most of the discomfort I see on the tee results from improper alignment. The golfer is twisted, ever so slightly, and doesn't feel right. If you are not comfortable, back off and start again.

j. Body scan. Release any tension in your body.

Mental Approach—Use the exercise you learned in the last two chapters.

k. Waggle the club. Waggle the club to preview your full swing.

Mental Approach—Ben Hogan has said that the waggle is a preview swing: if you waggle quickly, your swing will be fast; if you waggle slowly, your swing will be slow.

The waggle sets the stage for the actual swing. During the waggle several things happen: you preview the path the club will take, you preview the pace at which you will swing, you program the timing of your swing, you send the instructions for creating the shot from your brain to your muscles, and you adjust your setup so that the club comes squarely through the ball when you take your golf swing. Obviously, the waggle varies from shot to shot, since it is a mini-swing of the shot you are creating, which isn't the same for every situation. For instance, you may take a long, flowing waggle for a full swing on the tee and a shorter waggle for a 60-yard pitch shot.

l. The forward press. Do your forward press to initiate the movement of your swing.

Mental Approach—I favor using a forward press to get your body in motion. Whatever you select as your forward press—moving your hands forward, moving your right knee in, or cocking your head back—do it every time you swing the club.

Execution
After the forward press, simply take the club back and let the swing happen as planned.

Mental Approach—You have followed all the steps. Now just let your golf swing happen.

Debriefing
Depending on the success of your golf shot, you should take a debriefing swing. Mentally reinforce a swing with which you are happy or reprogram the correct swing after you have made a mechanical error. The debriefing swing in this case is a timing swing.

SKULL PRACTICE: LEARNING THE MENTAL SKILLS—AUTOGENIC TRAINING
Autogenic training is a relaxation technique that uses exercises to bring about the

sensations of body warmth and heaviness* in the limbs and torso, then uses relaxing images to expand this physical relaxation to the mind. "Autogenic" means "self-generating"—you do the procedure yourself—and these exercises are essential training in self-hypnosis. Have you ever been driving along a highway and suddenly realized that the exit you were looking for was two exits back? This kind of daydreaming is a form of trance. Hypnosis is simply a deeper trance. Remember, you are in charge: you put yourself in a trance, you do only the behavior that you want to do, and you wake yourself up.

Two physical sensations are experienced during hypnosis: general body warmth and heaviness or lightness in the limbs and torso. The warmth is a function of the blood vessels dilating, resulting in increased blood flow. The heaviness is a function of the muscles relaxing.

Both autogenic training and meditation lead to a state of relaxation, but they get there by different routes. Meditation gets there by using the mind to relax the body; autogenic training uses the sensations of heaviness and warmth to relax the body and to expand this relaxed state to the mind using imagery. Imagery is the foundation for visualization.

Physiological effects of autogenic training include a decrease in: heart rate, respiration, muscle tension, and serum cholesterol levels. Several illnesses are aided by autogenic training, including migraine headaches, Raynaud's disease, substance abuse and addiction, insomnia, and hypertension. Some additional applications of autogenic training include bronchial asthma, constipation, writer's cramp, indigestion, ulcers, hemorrhoids, tuberculosis, diabetes, and lower back pain.

Psychological effects include a reduction in anxiety and depression, a decrease in tiredness, and an increase in resistance to stress. Autogenic training can also help people suffering from pain associated with chronic illness.

Autogenic training

1. Sit or lie down in a comfortable position.

2. Close your eyes and take a slow, deep breath.
   Inhale as much air as you can.
   Exhale slowly and completely allowing the tension to leave your body.
   Just let the air come out by itself. ***

3. Take another deep breath and let it out. ***

---

* Most people experience heaviness with profound relaxation, while others experience lightness. Those who experience heaviness feel that, during relaxation, their legs and arms are so heavy they cannot pick them up. Those who experience lightness feel as if they are floating on a cloud. You will have to experiment. Go with the feeling that comes more naturally. There is no right or wrong way to feel.

4. Take a few more breaths. Say the word "relax" each time you exhale. ***

5. Relax your arms. ***

6. Relax your facial muscles. ***
   Relax your forehead, your eyes, your jaw, your tongue. ***

7. Relax your neck and shoulder muscles. ***

8. Relax your upper back and stomach. ***

9. Relax your legs. ***

10. Relax your entire body. ***

11. Let go of any tension that you may have in your body.

12. Take a deep breath and allow these parts of your body to relax even more. ***
    Continue to breathe normally and relax. ***
    Notice that each time you breathe out you relax deeper and deeper. ***
    Each time you breathe, relax more deeply. (*pause* for 30 seconds)

13. Repeat the following phrases to yourself:
    I am quiet. ***
    I am calm. ***
    I am relaxed. ***
    My right arm is warm (repeat three times). ***
    My right arm is heavy (repeat three times). ***
    My right arm is heavy* and warm. ***
    My left arm is warm (repeat three times). ***
    My left arm is warm (repeat three times). ***
    My left arm is heavy (repeat three times). ***
    My left arm is heavy and warm. ***
    Both my arms are heavy and warm.
    My right leg is warm (repeat three times). ***
    My right leg is heavy (repeat three times). ***
    My right leg is heavy and warm. ***
    My left leg is warm (repeat three times). ***
    My left leg is warm (repeat three times). ***
    My left leg is heavy (repeat three times). ***
    My left leg is heavy and warm. ***
    Both my legs are heavy and warm. ***
    My heart is calm and relaxed (repeat three times). ***
    My breathing is regular. ***

* If you prefer the feeling of lightness, replace the word "heavy" with the word "light."

My breathing is calm. ***
My breathing is calm and relaxed (repeat three times). ***
My solar plexus (or abdomen—stomach) is warm (repeat three times). ***
My forehead is cool (repeat three times). ***
I am calm. ***
I am relaxed. ***
I am quiet. ***

14. I am very relaxed (repeat three times). ***

15. Memorize these feelings of freedom, relaxation, and goodness, knowing that you can learn to achieve these feelings any time you want to.
     (*Pause* for 30 seconds).

16. Count backward from 5 to 1. During that time you can wake yourself up and when you wake up, you will feel relaxed and refreshed, alert and alive and good in every way. 5 *** 4 *** 3 *** 2 *** 1.

INTEGRATION EXERCISES—GETTING YOUR MIND AND BODY TO WORK AS A UNIT

Exercises to improve fundamentals
The grip. One way of discovering the feel of the correct grip and grip pressure is to hold your golf club in front of you at a 45-degree angle, with the clubhead facing the sky. This puts your golf club in your hands in the correct position and also indicates how much pressure is needed to hold the club. Hold and grip a golf club about a dozen times a day for a couple of weeks to learn this feeling.

The setup. The way to relate your target line and body alignment is to use the "railroad track" exercise. In this exercise you can use two golf clubs, two boards, or two one-inch square sticks. Whichever you choose, place one track parallel to your target line about 3 inches on the outside (far side) of your golf ball. The other track is placed parallel to the first and in line with your toes. Your intermediate target is in line with your golf ball and parallel to these two tracks. Your toes, knees, hips, and shoulders should all be parallel to the lines made by these sticks. Use a full-length mirror to see whether you are set up correctly, or use a video tape to tape your approach to the ball. You may want to videotape your practice session and view how you are setting up to the ball. In the first couple of sessions I would recommend concentrating only on your setup. Later you can hit balls from this position.

Many golfers get in the habit of compensating for deficiencies in their setup or swing. Someone may set up correctly but always hit the ball in the left rough because of some minor problem with her grip or equipment. To compensate for this she may begin to aim right so their golf ball ends up in the middle of the fairway. In time she may add a few more compensations until she finds herself wondering why she is no longer consistent. What she needed was some professional help from a local golf pro, who would have shown her how to deal with a minor problem instead of making compensations.

Distance assessment. At some point you will want to know the average distance you hit a golf ball with each club. Notice that I didn't say how far you *can* hit a golf ball with each club but how far you hit the golf ball on average. Sure, many golfers can strike the golf ball and send it 8 to 12 yards farther than their usual distance, but this takes excessive effort. Excess effort usually breaks down your swing if you try to do it repeatedly. Your timing speeds up, your rhythm is disrupted, and your pace is thrown out of kilter. What you need to do is determine how far you can send the golf ball using 80 percent of your power. Then you need to use this 80 percent power as your standard effort.

Go to a practice range—a football field with lines every 10 yards is perfect—and hit some 9 iron shots. Mark down your average distance in your record book. Then take your 8 iron and repeat the drill. Work your way through as many clubs as you can.

Next, go on the golf course for a practice round. You don't need to be concerned about score. In fact, don't keep score. Don't even putt any balls that you put on the green. Pace off your drives and your 3 woods. Hit a couple of balls from the 150-yard marker. Hit a couple of balls from various other distances. Mark down your distances for each club.

At the end of this exercise you will have sufficient knowledge of the average distance you hit a golf ball with each club. You may even have learned about the 80 percent effort rule.

The 80 percent rule. Take your 5 iron to the practice range. Do your normal warmup. I want you to hit 30 golf balls. Hit your first 5 balls using your regular swing. Observe where they land. Notice the distance as well as the direction. Hit the next five balls with your full swing using 90 percent effort. Notice the landing pattern. Hit the next five balls using your full swing with 80 percent effort and notice the landing pattern. Hit the next five balls using your full swing and 70 percent effort. What happened? Hit the last 10 balls using the 80 percent rule.

At some point in this exercise, you will use less effort than is productive. This is probably the 70 percent effort. This exercise should teach you that there is an optimum effort that is about 80 percent of your full effort. With this effort you have the greatest chance of optimizing your timing and pace, allowing all of your body parts to move in the correct sequence. As a result you will hit the golf ball farther and straighter. If you need less distance, select a more lofted golf club; don't use less effort. If you need more distance, select a less lofted golf club; don't try to kill a more lofted club. Don't succumb to the macho lure of demonstrating that you can hit the golf ball the same distance as everyone in your foursome with a lower iron. Another lesson to be learned from the 80 percent rule is that proper timing is essential.

Weight exercise. The weight exercise from chapter 4, "Execution," is worth repeating here. Remember, the purpose of this exercise was to allow you to feel the parts of your body "kick in" during your swing. If you swing too fast, you will get twisted because you won't be strong enough to control your swing and stop your golf club; if you swing too slow, you won't feel the rhythm.

Take your 3 wood and lead tape to the driving range and follow these instructions.

1. Take your 3 wood and apply some lead tape behind or on top of the clubhead. Increase the swing weight of the club by 3 to 4 swing-weights (D3 or D4 for men and D0 or D1 for women).

2. Without using a golf ball, pick a spot of grass over which to let your golf club travel. Address this area.

3. Take a nice, slow, easy swing back and stop at the top.

   ❑ Were you able to feel the club activate parts of your hands and arms?

   ❑ Did you notice anything about your grip? Try it again, paying attention to your grip.

   ❑ Did you have to grip the club more tightly?

   ❑ Were you able to feel your backswing?

   ❑ Did the clubhead feel heavier at the top?

4. Take your backswing another half-dozen times and see how it feels. Become aware of how it feels and memorize those feelings.

5. Once you have completed the backswing drill, take a full swing using the grass as the area over which you want your club to travel. How did it feel?

   ❑ Was your pace faster or slower?

   ❑ Did you feel your body react to the club?

   ❑ Did the slower pace help you to make a weight shift?

   ❑ Did you feel that the club was giving you kinesthetic cues that helped your pace?

6. Now tee up a ball and take a full swing using this new pace.

   ❑ Did your swing feel the same as when you did not have a ball in front of you?

144

❑ How was the ball flight?

❑ Did it differ from usual with the increased swing-weight of the 3 wood?

❑ Was the trajectory the same or different?

7. Hit another dozen balls and see if there is an improvement in your timing.

8. Did the weight change your pace? If it did, than you have benefited from the drill.

9. If you found this drill helpful, include it in your practice routine perhaps once every four times you practice.

Programming the "feel" of the swing. The best way to program the "feel" of the swing is to start with shots close to the hole. Go to the practice chipping green and chip some balls to the cup. Keep moving away from the green until you can no longer chip balls and you need to begin pitching.

Move to the pitching range and pitch some 30-yard pitches followed by some 50-yard pitches and some 70-yard pitches. If you can, hit some 90-yard pitches. You'll probably use the 11 o'clock position.

Move to the practice range and hit some full 9 iron shots, working your way down to the 3 iron or 4 iron. This should give you a feel for distance, effort, and timing.

The change of direction exercise. Although most teaching professionals will tell you not to stop at the top of your backswing, most will admit that there is a slight pause before changing direction. After all, if you are going backward and then change direction to go forward, the laws of physics dictate that you must stop somewhere.

With your 7 iron, take a few practice swings and hit a few balls. When you are comfortable hitting, start your normal swing and stop at the top of your backswing. Once you feel yourself stop, take your forward swing. You should be able to stop 5 or 10 seconds without disrupting your swing. If you need a timing sequence to this, you might take the club back and say "set," then say "through" on your forward swing.

Exercises to promote relaxation

Warmth exercise. Sit or lie down in a comfortable position. Pay attention to your breathing. With each breath, release tension from your body. When your body is sufficiently relaxed, focus on feeling warmth in your arms and legs.

Staircase exercise. Sit or lie down in a comfortable position. Pay attention to your breathing. With each breath, release tension from your body. When your body is sufficiently relaxed, imagine yourself at the top of a staircase and walk down the

145

staircase until you are as relaxed as you desire. Stay at that relaxed state for a couple of minutes and then return to your normal activity.

Tune out exercise. Repeat the second exercise. This time, when you are in the relaxed state you desire, listen to sounds. Listen, then tune them out. Pay attention to smells. Smell the different scents, then tune them out. When you have done each of these several times, return to your regular activity.

SECTION D:

FUELING FOR THE WHOLE NINE
YARDS: GETTING IN SHAPE

"My theory is that if you buy an ice-cream cone and
make it hit your mouth, you can play. If you stick it
on your forehead, your chances are less."
— *Vic Braden*
Tennis Instructor

In section A, I discussed strategies to be used prior to a round of golf and strategies to be used on the course during play. Section B was designed to help you get organized in your approach to striking the golf ball. Section C included some fundamentals and a mental approach to help you to learn and apply these fundamentals.

Now that you have had time to improve your approach to golf and have lowered your golf scores, we need to discuss the essential ingredients for peak performance in golf: physical fitness, mental fitness, and emotional fitness. Chapter 9, Sports Nutrition, will provide you with basic information about nutrition and will give you some sensible guidelines. To perform consistently well, you need to supply your body with a consistent supply of nutrients. Chapter 10, Sports Fitness, is about building a "machine" that will promote alertness, confidence, strength, and flexibility. These factors are important for success. If you want to play well, you need to have as much energy and endurance walking down the 18th fairway as you had walking down the first.

THE DIETER'S RATIONALIZATION DIET

Breakfast:
1 orange
1 slice whole wheat toast
1 glass of 2% milk

Lunch:
4 oz. broiled chicken breast (without the skin)
1 cup steamed carrots
1 chocolate chip cookie
1 cup of herb tea

Mid-afternoon snack:
Rest of the package of chocolate chip cookies
1 quart of Ben and Jerry's ice cream
1 jar of hot fudge

Dinner:
1 loaf of garlic bread
Large double-cheese pizza
3 Snickers candy bars
Entire frozen cheesecake eaten directly from the freezer

DIET TIPS

1. If no one sees you eat it, it doesn't have any calories.

2. If you drink a diet soda with a candy bar, they cancel each other out.

3. When you eat with someone else, calories don't count if you eat the same amount.

4. Food used for medicinal purposes never counts.

5. If you hang out with fatter people, you will look thinner.

6. Entertainment-related foods don't count—they are part of the entertainment experience.

7. Cookie pieces contain no calories. The process of breakage destroys the calories.

CHAPTER 9:

SPORTS NUTRITION: ADDING FUEL

TO THE FIRE

Two years ago an LPGA touring pro called me to help her improve her concentration. During our first session, I asked her about her concentration problem. She said, "I lose concentration about the 14th or 15th hole." I asked her if this loss of concentration occurred every time she played golf or if it were a hit-and-miss occurrence. She said it was "pretty consistent, but not always." She also asked if I could give her some exercises to improve her concentration.

I explained to her that many factors affect concentration and that we would deal with each of them. As a typical background check I asked her if she had any medical problems, if she were married, if she had any family problems, if she had any problems with friends, why she chose golf as a career, what kind of diet she followed, what exercise program she followed, what her goals were, and how she felt about losing and winning.

After getting answers to these questions, I gave her the following "homework."

❑ List qualities that you like about yourself.

❑ Describe how you want to play golf.

❑ What barriers do you see that prevent you from playing this way?

❑ Keep a diary of play—times you played golf, whom you played with, and concentration lapses.

❑ Keep a diary of your diet—breakfast, lunch, dinner, and snacks.

❑ Keep a diary of unresolved conflicts with family and friends.

On Friday of the following week she returned with some valuable information. She had played golf five mornings, Saturday, Sunday, Tuesday, Wednesday, and Thursday. She had lost concentration two days, Tuesday and Thursday. I asked if she suspected any cause for the lapse of concentration on those two days and she said that she had no idea. I asked if there were any problems with her personal life, and she said no. I then asked to see her diet log. On Saturday, Sunday, and Wednesday, she ate toast, juice, and eggs. For breakfast on Tuesday and Thursday, she had chocolate-covered donuts from a nationally known chain of donut shops.

BREAKFAST SUMMARY

Day	Breakfast	Performance
Saturday	Toast etc.	Good
Sunday	Toast etc.	Good
Tuesday	Doughnut	Poor
Wednesday	Toast etc.	Good
Thursday	Doughnut	Poor

I asked her whether she thought that the chocolate-covered doughnuts and the loss of concentration were related. She smiled somewhat doubtfully and said she didn't know. She told me she didn't know much about nutrition. I explained that eating food with a high simple sugar content creates a high blood-sugar followed by a low blood-sugar several hours later. This would coincide with the time that she would be playing the 14th or 15th hole. Low blood-sugar usually means a lower level of concentration. She was amused but not convinced. I asked her to do an experiment. She would eat a breakfast consisting only of complex carbohydrate such as oatmeal or wheat. She could have hot or cold cereal or a prepared carbohydrate such as english muffins, bagels, or toast. She was to keep a diary and return to report any lapse in concentration.

This sugar "high" and sugar "low" is well documented in nutrition journals, in psychological journals, and in corporate literature. Employers are well aware of the decrement in productivity of their employees when they eat "sugar" breakfasts. These employees usually run to the coffee and donut table at about 10:30 am and get a surge of energy, which is later followed by a "down" period. Afternoons are usually their low productivity period (3:00 pm).

The next week my LPGA client returned and this time reported no lapse in concentration. She had become quite interested in the relationship between nutrition and performance. She even wanted to know about the effects of exercise. Of course, eliminating chocolate-covered doughnuts helped alleviate the her lapses in concentration, but this is a fairly simple solution to the complex problem of sports nutrition. Starting a healthful diet improves all aspects of sport— concentration, confidence, endurance, energy, outlook, and mental attitude. This is precisely the approach I take with all my clients, although they think that are coming to me only for mental skills training. You see, you really need a total program, not just a pep talk.

I don't believe you can completely separate the mental and the physical in an real of life, including golf. If you want to be consistent and successful, you need to have a healthful lifestyle, especially a healthful diet. With this in mind, let's look at some important points about sports nutrition.

THE GOAL OF NUTRITION

Why do you eat? Is it because you enjoy food? Do you eat to supply your body with nutrients for health and energy? Do you eat to compensate for psychological states such as sadness, anger, or frustration? Many people choose foods out of habit or on a whim rather than for what their bodies need for energy and health. As we become happier with ourselves and our bodies, we choose foods more appropriate to our goals of health and fitness.

Good nutrition means providing your body with nutrients to enhance health and performance by promoting the optimal functioning of your body. Good nutrition fuels your body with energy to train and perform well. On the other hand, poor nutrition weakens an athlete by denying him or her the energy needed for success.

So our nutritional goal is to feel good, to supply our bodies with nutrients for health, and to make sure we have the energy to work, play, and have fun.

THE PROCESS: FROM EATING FOOD TO USING ENERGY

Our bodies are composed of thousands of chemical compounds. These compounds can be manufactured from thirty-eight essential nutrients, providing there is a source of energy. The thirty-eight essential nutrients consist of fifteen minerals, eleven vitamins, ten amino acids, one fatty acid, and water.

The food we eat contains the building blocks for growth, maintenance, repair, protection, and energy production. There are three main classes of foods: *carbohydrate, fat,* and *protein*. Each of these is digested and broken down into the basic building blocks: *glucose, fatty acids,* and *amino acids,* respectively.

A typical meal contains a combination of these three main classes of foods. Carbohydrates are broken down to simple sugars (glucose) and absorbed into our blood. *Blood sugar* is then used for energy or converted into complex carbohydrate (glycogen) to be stored in our muscles and liver. When we exercise, glycogen is reconverted into blood sugar and used.

The fats we eat in a typical meal are broken down to fatty acids, which are then converted into molecules called *triglycerides*. Triglycerides are stored in adipose (fat) cells, ready to be processed for energy as needed.

The proteins in our meal are broken down into amino acids and used for synthesizing protein substances such as muscle, connective tissue, hormones, and enzymes, which help various other physiological processes. Excess amino acids are excreted, since there is no storage mechanism for them.

The next time we eat, the process starts all over. Our body weight reflects the balance between the number of calories* consumed and the number of calories burned through metabolism. When our caloric intake exceeds our caloric outflow, our bodies store the excess calories as fat. When outflow exceeds intake, we lose weight.

As our level of activity increases, our bodies call upon stored energy for fuel. This fuel can be either carbohydrate (blood glucose) or fat (free fatty acids). When we are at rest, both are used equally. As the *intensity* of our activity increases, our muscles become increasingly dependent on carbohydrate. Fat is less efficient than carbohydrate and cannot be used for maximal effort.

THE BASIC BUILDING BLOCKS

Carbohydrates

Carbohydrates are organic compounds† that consist of various sugar molecules. *Simple carbohydrates* are composed of one or two individual sugar molecules, which are not chemically bonded together. *Complex carbohydrates*, or starches, are composed of many individual sugar molecules chemically bonded together. Simple carbohydrates are very easily digested into glucose (blood sugar). Complex carbohydrates are composed of a long string of sugar molecules and are digested more slowly.

An abundant supply of carbohydrates is found in fruit, vegetables, grains, and beans. When these foods are eaten, they are broken down into glucose. This glucose is absorbed into the blood and transported to different areas of your body to be used for energy production,‡ or converted to glycogen and stored.

Glycogen is stored in your muscles and your liver, but space is limited. All the muscles in your body store only enough glycogen to provide 480 calories, less than what is needed to run one hour. Your liver stores 280 calories and your blood another 80. The total supply of calories stored as glycogen in your muscles and liver is sufficient to provide you with energy for twelve hours of rest or a little more than one hour of maximum exercise.

---

* A calorie is the amount of energy required to raise the temperature of one gram of water one degree centigrade.

† Organic compounds are compounds that come from living things. They include glucose, fructose, amino acids, and fatty acids. Inorganic compounds include sodium chloride, or table salt.

‡ An exception to this rule is that the sugar *fructose* is absorbed as is and is then transported to the liver for conversion to glucose.

154

When your body needs energy, glycogen is converted back to blood sugar in the muscles or liver. One gram of glucose provides four calories of energy.

After exercise or other activity, we need to replenish our carbohydrate stores. Diets composed of *complex* carbohydrate provide us with a significantly higher muscle glycogen within a 48-hour period after exercise.

Recommendation for golfers: Carbohydrates

❑ Carbohydrates are the best energy source for sports. The intensity, duration, and frequency of exercise determines the energy source required. Increased intensity means a shift from fats to carbohydrates for energy supply, although as your physical conditioning improves, you have a greater capacity to use fats.

❑ Your diet should consist of 65 to 70 percent carbohydrates. High-carbohydrate diets are best for athletes as well as more sedentary types.

❑ Complex carbohydrates provide you with the most consistent energy supply without taxing your pancreas.

❑ Complex carbohydrates do not cause sugar "highs" and "lows," with the resulting impairment in your ability to concentrate and make decisions.

❑ Foods rich in complex carbohydrates are grains (oatmeal, pasta, bread), vegetables, and beans.

❑ Fruit contains fructose. Although fructose is a simple sugar, it takes time to break down the storage compartments in the fruit so that the fructose can be absorbed into your blood and travel to your liver to be converted to glucose. For this reason, fruit acts like a complex carbohydrate and does not produce a high-and-low sugar effect.

Fats

Fats are organic compounds consisting of fatty acids. There are two kinds of fatty acids: saturated and unsaturated. The unsaturated fatty acids are further divided into mono-unsaturated and polyunsaturated fatty acids. Saturated fats are solid at room temperature. Unsaturated fats are liquid at room temperature.

Saturated fatty acid comes from animal fat. It is called "saturated" because each carbon atom contained in the molecule has the maximum number of hydrogen atoms attached to it; the molecule is "full" of hydrogen atoms. This kind of fatty acid has been linked to cardiovascular disease.

Mono-unsaturated fatty acids come from vegetable oils such as olive oil. Their carbon atoms have less than the "full" amount of hydrogen atoms attached to them.

Polyunsaturated fatty acids come from vegetable oils such as corn oil, safflower oil, and sunflower oil. They consist of a string of unsaturated fatty acid molecules. Mono-unsaturated and polyunsaturated fats are believed by some to be healthful, because their consumption has been linked to a reduction of those fatty acids connected with cardiovascular disease.

Meat, milk, and oils all contain fats. During digestion, the fats you eat are broken down into fatty acids and absorbed into your blood stream, where they travel as triglycerides—glycerol and fatty acids linked together. Fats are stored in your body in adipose, or fat, cells.

When your body needs energy, stored fatty acids can be released. A gram of fat provides you with 9 calories of energy.

Recommendations for golfers: Fats

❑ Fats are an important source of energy because they spare the limited carbohydrate energy.

❑ Your diet should consist of 15 to 20 percent fats.

❑ Of this 15 to 20 percent, less than one-third should be saturated fat, one-third mono-unsaturated fat, and one-third polyunsaturated fat. If you are going to move in one direction or another from this recommendation, I would reduce the saturated fat rather than either of the unsaturated fats.

❑ Fats provide a consistent supply of energy, although it takes 20 to 30 minutes of exercise to mobilize them for energy production.

❑ Higher physical fitness improves your ability to use fat as a source of energy.

❑ I advise my clients to limit their intake of saturated fats and to use vegetable oils as much as possible. Even your intake of unsaturated fats should be limited. Be very careful using saturated oils, since the result is somewhat like eating animals fats, which you want to avoid. Vegetable oils are sometimes saturated to give them a solid form, such as margarine.

Proteins

Proteins are organic compounds that consist of various units of amino acids. There are 22 amino acids, eight of which are essential, that is, cannot be synthesized by the human body. Some foods contain all eight essential amino acids, while others do not. Animal protein contains all eight. Vegetable protein, such as legumes (beans), nuts, grains, and seeds are low in one or more essential amino acids. If you do not eat animal protein, you need to eat a variety of other foods to ensure that you are receiving all the essential amino acids.

During digestion, protein foods are broken down into amino acids, then used for manufacturing connective tissue, hormones, and enzymes. Excess amino acids are excreted in your urine.

Protein does not provide energy except during times of starvation. However, the energy supplied by protein is 4 calories per gram.

Recommendations for golfers: Protein

❑ Protein is not ordinarily used as a source of energy.

❑ Your diet should consist of 15 percent protein and should include a variety of protein sources.

❑ Any protein consumed in excess of daily requirements is excreted in your urine.

Each of the following provides the necessary protein for a 150 pound person:
    Two ounces of protein
    Nine ounces of poultry, meat, fish, cheese, or peanut butter.
    Two cups of cottage cheese.
    Nine eggs.
    Three pints of milk.
    Four cups of beans.

SUMMARY OF FOOD CLASSES

Class	Calories	Storage	Diet %
Carbohydrates	4 cal/g	small	65-70%
Fat	9 cal/g	large	15-20%
Protein	4 cal/g	none	15%

Water

Water is the single most important nutrient. Our bodies are two-thirds water and require two quarts of water daily. Two-thirds of our intake is taken as liquid, and the remaining third is contained in the food we eat. We also excrete two quarts of water a day, two-thirds in our urine and one-third in sweat and water vapor carried by exhaled air.

Water helps rid us of excess heat during exercise. That is why even mild dehydration impairs performance. We tire easily and our strength is reduced. In the case of pronounced dehydration, blood pressure is decreased, our kidneys become damaged, and we may suffer from heat exhaustion or heat stroke.

Some signs of dehydration are:

❑ Heat cramps: Thirst, chills, clammy skin, throbbing heart beat, nausea.

❑ Heat exhaustion: Reduced sweating, dizziness, headache, shortness of breath, weak, rapid heart beat, lack of saliva, extreme fatigue.

❑ Heat stroke: Lack of sweat, dry, hot skin, lack of urine, hallucinations, swollen tongue, deafness, visual disturbances, aggression, unsteady walking, excessively high body temperature.

Sports drinks

Sports drinks are enjoying a high degree of popularity. They contain water, sugar, salt, and added flavoring. While sports drinks won't hurt exercisers, they usually don't help enhance performance, except in exercise routines lasting over ninety minutes. In these longer exercise periods your body runs out of glycogen, and replacing carbohydrate helps to give you a consistent flow of energy. A complication of sports drinks is that they usually contain too much sugar and usually the wrong kind of sugar. If you decide to drink sports drinks, a good rule of thumb is to dilute any drink that contains more than eight percent sugar and select a drink that is rich in fruit sugars.

Recommendations for golfers: Water

❑ Monitor your fluid loss by weighing yourself before and after exercise (one pound = one pint of water).

❑ Replace 50 percent of your predicted loss to prevent heat injury. In Arizona, athletes are advised to drink one to two quarts of water every hour, depending on the temperature and the intensity of activity.

❑ Drink cool (not cold) water regularly and avoid liquids with high sugar content.

Vitamins and minerals

Vitamins are "helper" compounds that, with enzymes, allow certain chemical reactions to take place. Vitamins are classified as water soluble or fat soluble. The water-soluble vitamins are the B-complex vitamins (thiamine, riboflavin, pyridoxine, cobalamin, niacin, biotin, pantothenic acid, and para-amino benzoic acid) and vitamin C (ascorbic acid). Water soluble vitamins are readily excreted from your body.

Fat-soluble vitamins are vitamins A, D, E, and K and are retained by your body, usually in fat storage. Certain vitamins are important for energy production, including vitamin A (adrenal gland stimulant), B-complex (energy, metabolism, and muscle tone maintenance), vitamin C (anti-stress, digestion, healing), vitamin D (heart action, nervous system maintenance), and vitamin E (cardiovascular, muscle, and nerve maintenance).

Minerals are inorganic chemical substances necessary for life. They are parts of all cells, tissues, and organs and are found in most chemical compounds in your body, including enzymes, vitamins, and hormones. Minerals allow certain physiological processes to occur, such as muscle contraction, nerve impulse transmission, electrolyte balance, blood clotting, and heart rhythm.

Many athletes ask, "Does supplementation enhance performance?" Supplementation of specific vitamins or minerals can enhance performance, but *only* in cases in which there is a deficiency of that particular vitamin or mineral.

Recommendations for golfers: Vitamins and minerals

❑ Eating a balanced diet provides *all* the vitamins and minerals required for optimal health.

❑ Supplementing vitamins or minerals beyond the RDA (Recommended Daily Allowance) enhances neither health nor fitness.

❑ For those individuals who desire to take vitamins, moderate doses of vitamins are not harmful.

❑ If you are concerned about your diet or vitamins, you should see your physician or a registered dietitian.

❑ Many athletes are deficient in iron. Twenty-two to twenty- five percent of female athletes and ten percent of male athletes are deficient in iron. If you suspect a deficiency, request that your physician order the proper laboratory tests.

CREATING A BALANCED DIET

"The only way one can become proficient at anything is self- discipline and dedication. The people who succeed are the ones that really do not let personal feelings get in their way from giving their all in whatever they choose to do. The superstar golfers are people who are willing to do and give a little bit more than the others who do not succeed.

159

> "When I was growing up and learning to play golf and during my career, I wouldn't even drink a cup of coffee for fear that it might affect my nerve control to some degree."
>
> — *Byron Nelson*
> Professional Golfer

Now that I have made the bold statement that you can get all the nutrients you need for health and peak performance from a balanced diet, you are probably wondering: "What is a balanced diet?" Let's start with an understanding that good nutrition for health is good nutrition for sports performance. The requirement for a balanced diet is that you eat daily portions of each of the four main food groups: meat, dairy, fruits and vegetables, and cereals and breads. The following are some *guidelines* for eating a balanced diet:

❑ Eat a variety of foods. A varied diet will give you all the nutrients you need.

❑ Distribute your meals wisely. Three moderate meals a day is reasonable. If you choose, you can eat 4 to 6 smaller meals.

❑ Maintain your ideal body weight. Your ideal body weight can be determined from height-weight charts in most health books.

❑ Eat mostly complex carbohydrates. Complex carbohydrates offer a steady flow of energy.

❑ Eat plenty of fresh fruits and vegetables. These foods provide many of the vitamins and minerals you need.

❑ Eat plenty of fiber. High-fiber foods help to regulate bowel function. Irregularity can be a source of distraction and interfere with concentration.

❑ Choose your intake of fats carefully. Remember, a diet high in saturated fats is associated with cardiovascular disease. You may want to read the labels to find hidden saturated fats such as palm oil, coconut oil, or hydrogenated margarine.

THE PRE-GAME MEAL

Although some athletes do not have a routine they follow to warm up, practice, or play their sport, they usually have a ritual that they follow about their pre-game meal. Many eat things like raw meat, wheat germ, bottled water, or vitamins. Others will try to pack in foods that will give them extra energy. Well, the purpose of the pre-game meal is not to provide some magic potion to pump you up; it is to keep you from feeling hungry before or during the game.

Most sports nutritionists recommend that you avoid eating two hours before play. They suggest that the meal consist of complex carbohydrates, such as pasta. You should avoid a meal heavy in fats (hamburgers, french fries, fried chicken, or fried fish) because these take too long to digest; a meal heavy in fiber, since fiber increases mobility of the intestines and may make you uncomfortable; spicy foods, because they may give you indigestion; and foods heavy in simple sugars, because of the high-low blood sugar reaction.

NUTRITION MYTHS

There are many myths about nutrition that circulate among athletes. Some of these myths are harmless and may even have a temporary positive psychological effect on performance, while others are harmful and have a negative effect on health and performance. In the long run, none of these myths have any positive effects on performance.

Quick-energy myths

a. "Eating foods with a high simple sugar content just before competition will provide a burst of quick energy." Foods included in this group are honey, soft drinks, and sweets. This is not true because of the blood sugar high which is followed by the blood sugar low.

b. "Vitamins give you more energy." None of the 14 known vitamins provides any energy.

c. "Amphetamines provide more competitive energy." There is no evidence that amphetamines provide energy or improve performance. There is plenty of evidence that amphetamines are harmful. They cause an increase in blood pressure, heart rate, and metabolism and actually reduce energy over the course of the event.

Performance myths

a. "Drinking water during competition causes an upset stomach or slows you down." Not true. Drinking water during competition prevents you from getting dehydrated. Dehydration hurts performance.

b. "Muscle cramps are caused by inadequate salt intake." Nope. Cramps are caused by severe loss of water through sweating. Drinking water will

161

prevent such cramps. Salt tablets only aggravate them by drawing more water from your muscles and into your stomach.

c. "Eating steak and eggs before an event improves performance." Eating a high-protein, high-fat meal just before competition contributes little energy or performance enhancement. This kind of meal may cause upset stomach, indigestion, or nausea if eaten within a couple of hours of the match.

NUTRITIONAL IMPLICATIONS FOR GOLF

The nutrition information so far applies to any sport. With golf, however, we have some slight variables. Golf demands fine motor coordination, sharp thinking, decision making, and high concentration. Diets that increase excitability or produce excess relaxation are counter-productive. With golf we need a steady flow of energy that is not too high and is not too low. We especially don't want wide swings in energy.

With this in mind, we should avoid foods that are heavy in fats or simple sugars. We should also avoid alcoholic beverages while we are playing. I once had an amateur golfer come to me because he couldn't understand why he played well on the front nine and poorly on the back nine. I found out that his normal routine was to have a beer at the turn. I suggested he eliminate the beer and see what happened. He played both sides equally well when he tried this. However, he played golf to relax and to socialize. Because of this, he decided to forgo the improved play in exchange for the enjoyment of a beer on the turn.

SKULL PRACTICE: LEARNING THE MENTAL SKILLS—VISUALIZATION

> "What other people may find in poetry or art museums, I find in the flight of a good drive—the white ball sailing up into the blue sky, growing smaller and smaller, then suddenly reaching its apex, curving, falling, and finally dropping to the turf to roll some more, just the way I planned it."
>
> — *Arnold Palmer*
> Professional Golfer

Visualization is a technique to teach you how to create mental scenes and create mental states. These mental states can be used to review the feel of a golf shot or to preview a golf shot. This is especially important if you are faced with a difficult golf shot you have successfully executed in the past and want to recall the method or the feel of the shot, or if you have a golf shot you have never played and need to preview how the golf ball will go during execution. Visualization is an important and necessary skill if you want to be successful in golf.

During your visualization you should try to use as many of your senses as you can. For example, if you are visualizing a scene at the beach, you may want to include the smell of the salt water, the sound of the wind blowing past your ears, the warmth of the sun on your skin, the energy you have when you are at the beach, and the joy of being there.

Visualization exercise

In this exercise I will ask you to go to what psychologist Lars Unestahl calls "your mental room." This mental room could be a room in your house, the beach, a mountain hideaway, or anything else that you care to designate as your mental room. Your mental room will serve as a place where you can go mentally, within seconds, to relax, to influence your behavior, to rehearse a skill, a talk, or a presentation, to learn problem solving, to control physiological responses, to control pain, to manage stress, or to recover from injury. Take your time and enjoy the feelings and the benefits of this exercise. You should do this exercise twice a day, perhaps as soon as you wake up in the morning and again when you go to bed. Follow this procedure.

1. Get comfortable.

2. Close your eyes and take a long, slow, deep breath. ***

3. Take another deep breath and let it out. ***

4. Take a few more deep breaths. Say the word "relax" each time you exhale. ***

5. Relax your arms. ***

6. Relax your facial muscles. ***

7. Relax your neck and shoulders. ***

8. Relax your upper back and stomach. ***

9. Relax your legs. ***

10. Relax your entire body. ***

11. Let go of any tension you may have in your body. Just let go. ***

12. Take a deep breath and allow the parts of your body to relax even more. ***
    Continue to breathe normally and relax. ***
    Notice how each time you breathe out, you relax even more. ***

163

Each time you breathe, relax more deeply (pause for 30 seconds).
***

13. Allow your entire body to let go of any tension. ***
    Relax every part of your body. ***
    Let go of any thoughts or feelings except the feelings of relaxation.
    Breathe normally and relax deeper and deeper with each exhalation.
    ***
    Allow the feelings of warmth to flow over your body. ***

14. Now that you are completely relaxed, visualize yourself on the top of a
    long staircase. *** When you are ready, I want you to walk slowly down
    this staircase. *** With each step, allow yourself to go deeper into a state
    of relaxation. *** Go deeper and deeper into relaxation. *** As you slow-
    ly walk down the staircase and become more and more relaxed, you will
    come to a place that is very attractive to you, a place you feel will allow
    you to relax even more. *** When you find a comfortable place at the
    side of the staircase, you can get off and wait for further instructions.
    (Pause for 30 seconds.)

15. Now that you have found a comfortable place, look around until you find
    a door. *** This door is the entrance to your mental room. *** You will
    use this room to influence yourself and to allow good things to happen to
    you. When you are ready, open the door and enter your mental room.
    Look around the room and see the familiar elements of the scene you
    have chosen. *** Take a few minutes to decorate the room any way you
    want. *** You will probably want a comfortable chair or couch to sit in.
    *** You have the power and the imagination to set up your room in any
    way you see fit. ***

16. Sit or lie down in your comfortable chair or couch *** and feel the relaxa-
    tion and freedom from tension. *** Freedom from worries, freedom to be
    who you want to be, *** Freedom to do what you want to do. *** During
    the times when you decide to let someone else into your mental room,
    that person will accept you as you are: a happy, intelligent, warm, sensi-
    tive, and competent human being they love to be around.

17. Memorize the feelings you have in your mental room. *** Know that you
    can come back to your room anytime you want, *** To work on any
    changes you want to make in your own life, *** To practice any skills or
    behavior you may want to perfect.

18. In a minute I'm going to count backward from 5 to 1, and you can leave your
    room and return to where you are now. *** 5 *** 4 *** 3 *** 2 *** 1.

INTEGRATION EXERCISES—GETTING YOUR MIND AND BODY TO WORK AS A UNIT

Diet log. Keep a diet log for the next week. In your log, keep track of the following information:

    a. What you eat.

    b. What time you eat.

    c. How you feel before and after each meal.

    d. What time you get hungry.

    e. Your level of concentration during the day. Make a note if you find that you are losing concentration.

    g. Your energy level. Make a note when you realize your energy level is decreasing. Also mark down what you think of doing when you feel this lull in energy.

    Analysis of diet log. Look for a relationship between what you ate and your level of concentration and your level of energy. You are looking for the time span between what you ate and your mood. If you are eating too much refined sugar, you will see these events occurring within two to three hours after the meal.

    Analysis of compensations for concentration and/or energy. Look for the times that you felt your concentration diminishing or your energy decreasing. What did you think of doing at those times? Did you reach for a soft drink that contained caffeine or sugar? Did you think of eating again?

    Action plan. If you determined that your mood, energy, or concentration was affected by your dietary habits, you may want to modify what you eat or drink. Once you make these changes, do another diet log and see whether there is an improvement. Keep these logs for future reference. Do this slowly, because our bodies don't like fast or extreme changes.

CHAPTER 10:

SPORTS FITNESS: TUNING UP THE ENGINE

"My doctor recently told me that jogging could add years to my life. I think he was right. I feel ten years older already."

— Milton Berle
Comedian

During high school, I lived two blocks from the field where my high school football team practiced and I often walked to the field to watch. Some of the players practiced blocking by hitting against a "sled' with their shoulders. Some practiced throwing the football, while others practiced receiving it. At the end, the players would run laps. Practice seemed fairly routine.

The most interesting part of football practice was the coach. He was built a little like Jackie Gleason. During practice, you could find him standing on the sidelines dressed in his teaching clothes and open wind breaker, his hands in his pockets. He always had a ball of chewing tobacco in his mouth, and his "spit" timing had a rhythm of its own. He would occasionally call someone's name and order him to "take a couple of laps" or to "take a shower."

The team was periodically successful playing against other teams who were in the same boat as they were. The players were not athletes, only football players. They went out on the field and *played* football.

One year a fascinating development took place, one that would have a profound effect on my life, although I didn't realize it at the time. That year the regular coach became ill before the start of football season and had to take the year off from teaching and coaching. The school contracted a local businessman to coach the team. On the first day of practice the new coach appeared. He was tall, trim, and dressed in a gray sweat suit and sneakers. He carried a clipboard and looked like he meant business. His demeanor said he was "in charge." He assembled all the players and told them his plan for the season and his plan for the practice sessions. They were to start out with stretching exercises and calisthenics, followed by practice. Afterward, they would do laps before hitting the showers.

There was something really different here. You could feel the resentment of the older players, who thought, "We never did it this way before."

Well, the stretching began. Who do you think was in there leading the exercise? Right, the coach. He led the stretching and the calisthenics, and after practice, he led the players around the field and up and down hills. People were talking. Some of the comments went like this: "Who does this guy think he is? "He's nuts!" "I wonder if he knows anything about football."

I took a slightly different view. I thought the guy knew what he was doing. He had an energy and enthusiasm I had never seen before. Here was this guy training athletes, not just letting kids "play" football. Things were really different this year. I had never seen anything like this before. I was impressed.

By now you must be wondering, "How successful was the team that year?" It was their most successful season. But even if the season had not been successful in the number of games won, it would have been successful in teaching adolescents how to get organized, how to formulate goals, and how to achieve these goals. It would have taught them life-skills, which is what playing a sport is all about.

Well, you can play golf and enjoy the game without good physical fitness, without good health, and without the confidence that physical, mental, and emotional conditioning provides. You can, but golf won't feel as good as it would if you were fit. You won't feel as good as if you were fit.

Do the pros feel this way? Many do. When Jack Nicklaus and Lee Travino were approaching eligibility for the Senior Tour, guess who increased his exercise program? Gary Player. Player knew he had to spend more time on the bicycle and other kinds of exercises, and watch his diet more closely, because the caliber of play on the Senior Tour would be at a higher level with Nicklaus and Trevino coming aboard.

WHAT IS PHYSICAL FITNESS?

Physical fitness is the ability to recover quickly from strenuous activity. Since strenuous activity is accompanied by increased oxygen consumption, fitness requires an increased ability to handle oxygen. You must be able to breathe deeply, filling your lungs, and you must be able to transport oxygen from your lungs to every part of your body that needs it. For this you need an efficient pumping system which means that your heart is strong and your blood vessels are in good working order. Physical fitness is often called cardiorespiratory fitness, because your heart and lungs are the chief ingredients in the fitness recipe.

Does this sound like a lot of work? How much work do you suppose? How many hours a week would it take to achieve physical fitness? Five? Ten? Fifteen? Twenty? How much time would you be willing to spend on activities to keep you fit?

Good news. It would take about ninety minutes a week. That's right. One-and-a-half hours a week. Not bad when you consider that a week has 168 hours. But here's the catch, You can't do it all at once. You need 20 to 25 minutes four times a week. No problem? A piece of cake, you say! Good!

Physical fitness is important for an athlete. It gives him or her the ability to stay in control physically, mentally, and emotionally. If you need a little more motivation, read the next section about the benefits of exercise.

THE BENEFITS OF PHYSICAL FITNESS: AEROBIC EXERCISE

Aerobic exercise is exercise of relatively long duration (20 to 30 minutes) that uses the large muscle groups, demands no more oxygen than you can take in, and requires that your exercising heart rate (called "target heart rate") reach 60 to 70 percent of your maximum heart rate. More on this later.

Exercise provides physiological as well as psychological benefits.

Physiological benefits of aerobic exercise.

❑ It improves the function of the circulatory system by strengthening heart muscle, lowering pulse rate (fewer beats per minute), increasing stroke volume (more blood per contraction), increasing red blood cell production, helping to maintain normal blood pressure, decreasing low-density lipoprotein (LDL) associated with heart disease, and increasing high-density lipoprotein (HDL) which protects against heart disease.

❑ It improves the function of the lungs, providing them with greater elasticity to breathe.

❑ It results in quicker recovery time from strenuous activity.

❑ It increases endurance.

❑ It tones muscles.

❑ It burns calories to help you to maintain your ideal weight.

❑ It delays the degenerative changes of aging.

Psychological benefits of aerobic exercise

- ❏ It decreases anxiety and depression.

- ❏ It improves your mood.

- ❏ It improves self-esteem.

- ❏ It helps you to relax by reducing resting muscle tension.

- ❏ It helps you to handle psychological stress.

- ❏ It helps build confidence.

- ❏ The greatest psychological benefit comes from aerobic exercise at 70 to 80 percent of target heart rate for 25 to 30 minutes 4 to 5 times a week in activities such as brisk walking, running, swimming, or cross-country skiing.

EXERCISE—THE BASICS

Although the scope of this book limits specific recommendations for starting an exercise program, I do want to give you some guidelines that will help you to get to a "good" level of fitness.

Health assessment

As with any exercise program, you should make an appointment with your physician for a medical examination. This examination should include the following:

- ❏ Comprehensive health history

- ❏ Physical examination—including heart, lungs, eyes, skin, nervous system, abdominal, rectal, and breast examination and pap smear for women.

- ❏ Laboratory studies—including cholesterol profile, electrolytes, blood sugar, and complete blood count.

- ❏ X-rays.

- ❏ Cardiorespiratory evaluation on a treadmill.

Cardiorespiratory fitness

In people who are physically fit, the cardiovascular and respiratory systems are strong and highly efficient allowing them to sustain periods of strenuous activity.

a. Respiratory system. As you begin to increase your activity, whether work or exercise, your lungs begin to increase their activity, with a resulting increase in your oxygen intake. As your activity continues to increase, your intake of oxygen increases proportionately. Eventually, however, it levels off, that is, hits a maximum. This maximal intake level of oxygen is called "VO_2 max." VO_2 max varies from person to person depending on factors such as health, sex, age, physical condition, and size. The higher the VO_2 max, the better your physiological readiness for exercise. Through aerobic training you can increase your VO_2 max and your endurance for strenuous activity.

Are you concerned about being able to perform strenuous activity? Probably not. However, increasing your endurance for strenuous activity will also increase your stamina for routine activity.

b.   Cardiovascular system. The heart and circulatory system are the second group of key players in fitness. As you increase your activity your heart rate begins to increase to keep up with your body's increased demands for oxygen and sugar. Like the functioning of the lungs, your heart rate increases to a point, beyond which increased exercise intensity does not produce an increase in your heart rate. This point is called "maximum heart rate" and is analogous to VO_2 max. Maximum heart rate is used to design an aerobic exercise program. The goal of aerobic training is to lower your resting heart rate and to increase stroke volume of the heart so that it doesn't have to work as hard to pump the same amount of blood during strenuous activity. The heart essentially conserves energy.

Exercising your way to health
If you are serious about exercising, you probably have two main exercise goals: to be physically fit and to be healthy. Both fitness and health contribute to your performing well and feeling good. You may wish to secure an exercise prescription, an exercise program designed specifically for you by an athletic trainer. Such professionals take into account your physical condition and health as well as your fitness goals. The American College of Sports Medicine suggests that the goal of exercise prescription should be to exercise at sufficient intensity to produce improvements in performance and health, but not so vigorously as to cause cardiovascular problems.

Calculating your heart rate
Heart rate (HR) is a barometer of exercise activity and physical fitness. Because your heart rate increases with your intensity of exercise, you can monitor your exercise intensity by monitoring your heart rate. For example, if you want to exercise at moderate intensity and you know your peak heart rate, or maximum, you can calculate the heart rate at which to exercise—your target heart rate. Periodically, during exercise, you can take your pulse to check the relationship between your ac-

tual heart rate and your target heart rate. By doing this you will know if you are exercising at the intensity you desire.

Dr. Bruce Noble (Physiology of Exercise and Sport) describes the Karvonen method for calculating target heart rate. Let's walk through an example. I am going to calculate the target heart rate for several different exercise intensities for a 30-year-old.

1. Resting heart rate: Before you exercise, take your resting heart rate using the radial pulse in your wrist (thumb side with palm up).
    It should be around 60 to 80 beats per minute.
    Example: 80 beats per minute.

2. Calculate your peak heart rate using the following formula:
    Peak heart rate = 209 - 0.74 x your age (in years)
    Example: 209 - 0.74 x 30 = 185 beats per minute

3. Calculate your heart rate range (HRR) using the following formula:
    Heart rate range = Your peak heart rate - your resting heart rate
    Example: 185 - 80 = 100 beats per minute

4. Calculate your target heart rate for the following exercise intensities:
    General formula:
    Target HR = HRR x exercise intensity factor + resting heart rate.

    a) Target heart rate for light exercise intensity (50 percent)
    Target HR = 100 x 0.50 + 80 = 130 beats per minute

    b) Target heart rate for light moderate exercise intensity (60 percent)
    Target HR = 100 x 0.60 + 80 = 140 beats per minute

    c) Target heart rate for moderate exercise intensity (70 percent)
    Target HR = 100 x 0.70 + 80 = 150 beats per minute

    d) Target heart rate for heavy exercise intensity (80 percent)
    Target HR = 100 x 0.80 + 80 = 160 beats per minute

    e) Target heart rate for strenuous exercise intensity (90 percent)
    Target HR = 100 x 0.90 + 80 = 170 beats per minute

Listen to your body
If you are in tune with what your body is telling you, you are a smart exerciser. It is important to note that pain is not a challenge to overcome; it is a warning signal that something is wrong. Pain can be caused by a medical problem, improperly fitting athletic gear, an incorrectly planned exercise program, or simply overdoing it.

If you feel physically tired but mentally alert after exercising, you are probably going at exercise in an intelligent way. If you feel wiped out or "wrecked" afterward and you take a couple of days to recover, you may want to reevaluate your exercise program.

Approach to exercise
Whether you are exercising to improve physical fitness, to enhance health, to reduce stress or anxiety, or just to have fun, take some time to plan your exercise program. Most people start an exercise program at light intensity and work up to moderate exercise intensity over a period of 2 to 6 months. Remember, it is undesirable to exercise at strenuous exercise intensity, since the stress on the body outweighs the physical fitness benefits received. Moreover, you will probably not be able to exercise long enough (20 to 30 minutes) to achieve an aerobic benefit.

Most exercise enthusiasts in good health with no joint or muscle problems can exercise in the range of light or moderate to heavy exercise intensity. This kind of program will improve your physical fitness and enhance your health, ensuring that you will meet your goals. Choose an exercise or sport you like, and the physical activity you do will help you to become physically fit, improve your self-esteem, and give you the control you want in your life.

Choosing an activity
Select something enjoyable. Take into consideration your personal interests, skills, exercise goals, and exercise capacity.

Aerobic exercise activities that can help you to reach your goals of physical fitness include brisk walking, jogging, running, swimming, aerobic dance, and biking. All of these are considered high aerobic activities, except brisk walking, which is considered a moderate aerobic activity.

Whichever you choose, you have a greater likelihood of remaining in your exercise program if you set realistic goals, make these goals known to your spouse or friends, have someone with whom you can exercise, and start the program slowly.

Getting started
The first question to ask yourself is, "Do I want to exercise and increase my level of physical fitness?" If the answer is yes, I suggest you make a list of the benefits you expect to receive from exercise and another of the costs. An example of cost is time. What is another cost?

After you have gone to your physician for a physical, the next step is to visit an athletic trainer. He or she will help you to determine your physical fitness and your target heart rate and will help you to plan an activity program. The following discussion is for someone who has been sedentary and wants to start an exercise program.

Most people who are sedentary would start at the light (50 percent) or light moderate (60 percent) exercise intensity. This can be accomplished by brisk walking.

A self-test for fitness

Dr. Kenneth Cooper describes a method to determine your fitness level. Dr. Cooper's method is simply this: Walk, jog, or run on a measured track for a 12-minute period.

This table will tell you your approximate level of fitness.

DISTANCE	FITNESS LEVEL
< ¾ mile	Poor
¾ – 1 mile	Fair
1 – 1¼ miles	Good
1¼ – 1½ miles	Very good
1½ – 1¾ miles	Excellent
> 1¾ miles	Superior

Map out your walking program. You should walk the following distances during the week indicated:

WEEK	DISTANCE (miles)	TIME (minutes)	FREQUENCY (times per week)
1	1	35	3x
2	1¼	35	4x
3	1½	35	4x
4	1¾	35	4x
5	2	35	4x
6	2	32	4x
7	2	30	4x
8	2	27	4x
9	2	25	4x
10	2	23	4x

Once you have reached the brisk 2-mile, 23-minute walk, all you need to do is walk 3 or 4 times a week to maintain a "good" level of physical fitness. If you should desire a better than "good" level of fitness, there are many resources to guide you on this journey.

PHYSICAL FITNESS FOR GOLF

In addition to the general fitness exercises, you will want to do some stretching exercises to help your golf game. When I first began to exercise, I went to a physical therapist to learn about stretching exercises. Some of the exercises he taught me were for general flexibility, some were applicable to golf. Sports medicine consultants recommend that you perform stretching exercises before beginning any form of exercise or playing any sport.

The purpose for stretching is twofold. First, you want to prevent injury when your exercise or swing your golf club. Second, you want to be as flexible as possible in order to be able to swing the golf club in a maximum arc. To generate maximum clubhead speed, you must be able to turn your body with ease. Without this agility you will be forced to compromise with a less-than-full swing, which means a sacrifice of distance and accuracy. To develop agility you need to perform some simple stretching exercises. You may want to develop your own.

I use the following exercises before I go on the practice range or play golf. I hold each position for 10 to 15 seconds. Each of these movements should be done slowly to allow your muscles to stretch. Avoid a bouncing motion. The more you relax, the greater your ability to stretch. Just let it happen; don't force the movements.

❑ Touch your toes. With your legs shoulder-length apart, bend over from your waist and touch your toes. First your right hand touches your right toes and your left hand touches your left toes. Then you touch the toes of your opposite foot. If you cannot touch them yet, give it a few weeks; you will be able to eventually. As you become more flexible, you may be able to touch your heels.

❑ Reach for the sky. Reach with both arms at the same time, stretching your arms, chest and legs. Finish reaching on your toes.

❑ Reach in front of you. Bring your arms down until they are pointing forward. Reach out until you feel that your shoulders are coming forward.

❑ Reach out to the side. Move your arms from in front of you to the sides and reach as far to the left and the right as you can. Finish with your arms at your sides.

❑ Side stretch. With both arms at your sides, stretch your right arm overhead and slide your left arm down your left leg. Repeat with your left side.

❑ Body rotation. Take a golf club and put it on your shoulders with your hands over the top. Stand upright with your feet shoulder length apart. Rotate your body as far right as possible and then as far left as possible. Next, with the golf club in the same position over your shoulders, take your address position and rotate your shoulders as you would in your golf swing.

❑ Body action stretch. Take your golf club and take a couple of mini-swings, programming your body to get you into the athletic position—right knee

175

is firm and pointing in and your left side is stretched—and to release from this position.

SKULL PRACTICE: LEARNING THE MENTAL SKILLS—PREVIEWING SPORTS PERFORMANCE

"I'm kind of in my own world out there. I do something called psychocybernetics 15 minutes a day, visualizing positive things, like sacking quarterbacks. By Sunday, I'm in a shell. I don't know names and faces, just the guy I have to beat."

—*Randy White*
Professional Football Player (tackle)

One of the most useful mental tools in golf is the ability to "see" a successful golf shot before it is executed. When you develop this ability, your golf score will improve dramatically. You will be able to see the golf ball during a successful shot, to determine which club will transform your picture into reality, to integrate the effort needed to produce the golf shot that you saw in your picture, and, if necessary to alter either your plan or your picture to achieve your goal.

In this relaxation exercise I will ask you to go to your mental room. When you get there, you will create a film screen on which to watch your performance. This exercise differs from the others in that you will watch yourself perform from outside your body. In the past you have visualized how your golf ball rolled on the green or how it flew through the air. These images were "seen" from inside your head through the window of your eye. This time you will see yourself standing on the green putting or standing in the fairway. It is effortless on your part because you just sit back and enjoy the show. Have fun!

1. Get comfortable.

2. Close your eyes and take a long, slow, deep breath. ***

3. Take another deep breath and let it out. ***

4. Take a few more deep breaths. Say the word "relax" each time you exhale. ***

5. Relax your arms. ***

6. Relax your facial muscles. ***

7. Relax your neck and shoulders. ***

8. Relax your upper back and stomach. ***

9. Relax your legs. ***

10. Relax your entire body. ***

11. Let go of any tension that you may have in your body. Just let go. ***

12. Take a deep breath and allow the parts of your body to relax even more. ***
    Continue to breathe normally and relax. ***
    Notice that each time you breathe out, you relax even more. ***
    Each time you breathe, relax more deeply (pause for 30 seconds). ***

13. Allow your entire body to let go of any tension. ***
    Relax every part of your body. ***
    Let go of any thoughts or feelings except for the feelings of relaxation.
    Breathe normally and relax deeper and deeper with each exhalation. ***
    Allow the feelings of warmth to flow over your body. ***

14. Now that you are completely relaxed, visualize yourself on the top of a long staircase. *** When you are ready, I want you to walk slowly down this staircase. *** With each step, allow yourself to go deeper into a state of relaxation. *** Go deeper and deeper into a state of relaxation. *** As you slowly walk down the staircase and become more and more relaxed, you will come to your mental place. *** (Pause for 30 seconds)

15. Go into your mental room and sit down on the comfortable chair. *** You will notice a film screen in front of you positioned so that you can see it easily. *** In a couple of minutes, the picture will begin and you will see yourself performing several golf shots. *** You will see yourself performing these golf shots perfectly *** flawlessly. *** Take your time watching the film and allow all of your senses to experience the performance. ***

16. Now you see the film beginning. *** You are on the number-one green of your favorite course. *** You have a four-foot putt. *** Watch as you assess your putt, looking at the green. *** Looking at the line the golf ball will take as it rolls to the cup. *** Watch yourself take a practice stroke. *** Watch as you successfully roll your golf ball to the center of the cup. *** Allow yourself to feel all the sensations of a truly good performance (pause for 60 seconds). Repeat your putt several times until you feel how good it is to be a great putter. *** (pause for 90 seconds)

177

17. Now you are on the next green and you have a 10-foot putt. *** Watch yourself as you approach the putt, examining all the elements you need to in order to be confident that you will roll the golf ball to the center of the cup. *** Watch yourself take a practice stroke. *** Watch yourself stroke the ball and roll it to the center of the cup. *** Feel the confidence that this performance give you. *** Repeat your putt several more times. *** (pause for 90 seconds)

18. Now you are on the fairway 110 yards from the green. *** Watch yourself as you evaluate the lie of the golf ball. *** Watch yourself as you assess your target area. *** Visualize the shot. *** You can see yourself select the correct golf club for your shot. *** You can see yourself taking a programming mini-swing. *** Watch yourself as you execute your golf shot. *** Watch the golf ball in flight. *** Watch it land softly on the green near the cup. *** Allow yourself to feel the good sensations that you have after executing a great golf shot. *** Know in your heart that you can perform this shot repeatedly on any golf course. Watch this golf shot several more times. *** (pause 90 seconds)

19. Now you are on the tee of the next hole. *** You evaluate your target area. *** Watch yourself tee the golf ball. *** See yourself take a programming swing for timing. *** You can see yourself swing your driver and strike the golf ball. *** Watch the ball fly down the middle of the fairway. *** See it land and roll. *** Notice the good feelings that you have about your drive. *** Notice the confidence that you can hit a good drive just by relaxing and swinging your golf club slowly and rhythmically. *** There is no need to force your swing. *** Your muscles know how to react to your golf swing. *** They know how to generate clubhead speed so that your golf ball goes in the correct direction and for the distance you desire. *** Repeat your drive several times. *** (pause for 90 seconds)

20. You have experienced a successful performance, a perfect performance that you previously thought was difficult. *** Memorize the feelings and thoughts you have right now. *** Enjoy the happiness you are feeling. *** Say to yourself, "I can do anything that I put my mind to." *** "I have the ability to play great golf." *** You have now programmed in your mind the sensations and feelings of success, sensations and feelings that are yours to keep forever. *** You have programmed yourself for success.

21. You now know what it is like to execute a task that you want to do successfully. *** You also know that you can reach a state of relaxation and go to your mental room any time you want to. In the beginning, you may

be more comfortable going through this process sitting or lying down with your eyes closed. But soon you will be able to do this exercise within seconds and with your eyes opened. *** You will be able to use your mental room on the golf course any time you want to preview a shot. ***

22. In a minute I'm going to count backward from 5 to 1 and you can wake yourself up. *** 5 *** 4 *** 3 *** 2 *** 1.

INTEGRATION EXERCISES—GETTING YOUR MIND AND BODY TO WORK AS A UNIT

Calculate your maximum heart rate. Using the formula and the example given earlier in this chapter, calculate your maximum heart rate. Assess the amount of intensity with which you would like to exercise and calculate 60 percent, 70 percent, and 80 percent of your maximum heart rate. These figures will be your target heart rates for when you exercise.

Working with your target heart rate. Before you exercise, take your resting heart rate. After 20 minutes of exercise, take your actual heart rate and see if it is close to your target heart rate. Brisk walking is ideal for this exercise.

Let's take an example. Suppose you want to exercise at about 70 percent of your maximum heart rate. You take a brisk two-mile walk and it takes you 30 minutes. During exercise you take your pulse and you notice that it is only 60 percent of your maximum heart rate. The next time, you have the option of walking the same course in less time, say, 25 or 27 minutes. With brisk walking it is very easy to adjust your effort simply by walking faster or slower. Later in your program you can increase your effort by walking with hand weights.

Identifying the actual benefits of exercise. Before you exercise, write down how you feel. Are your muscles tense? Are you happy? Do you feel energetic? After you exercise, I want you to answer the same questions again. Is there a difference in your answers? Are you getting immediate benefits?

SECTION E

GOLF PSYCHOLOGY: MAKING YOUR
MIND YOUR ALLY

"Many times when fear starts to get me, my best
chance of overcoming it lies in facing it squarely and
examining it rationally. Here's what I say to myself:
'O.K., what are you frightened of? You've obviously
played well overall. You're always telling yourself
you get your biggest kicks out of the challenges of
golf. Well, go ahead and enjoy yourself. Play each
shot one at a time and meet the challenge'."

— *Jack Nicklaus*
Professional Golfer

Elite athletes are in top physical condition. They approach their sport as seriously as physicians, lawyers, accountants, and other professionals approach their careers. Most of these professional athletes have diet, exercise, and practice programs to keep them alert, energetic, and confident.

Many professional golfers fall into the category of elite athletes. They are trim, fit, and energetic—in top physical condition. Now then: if we took a group of professional golfers, all equally trained in golf fundamentals and equally skilled, what would separate the more successful from the less successful? What would determine who would win on any particular day? The golfer with the best mental skills would win. It is the mental skills that separate the more successful golfers from the less successful golfers. This is true, of course, for all sports.

In this last section I will discuss mental and emotional conditioning. In chapter 11, Peak Performance, I will teach you psychological skills that can give you the edge when you are playing among your peers. These skills include developing confidence, improving concentration, and identifying and maintaining your optimal arousal state for peak performance.

In chapter 12, Managing Stress on the Golf Course, I will teach you how to make stress your ally. Successfully managing stress will reduce anxiety and tension and will help you to develop and display your natural talent.

CHAPTER 11:

PEAK PERFORMANCE IN GOLF: HOW

TO PLAY YOUR BEST

"Problems usually aren't as complicated as we make then. Adversity can be good for you. It can make you get off your fanny and get to work. A problem is an educational opportunity in disguise if you look at it constructively. There are a lot of potential lessons in any difficulty. I don't feel that I ever reach bottom when I get down. I get down so far and then it's like an extra motor fires up and I fight back."

—*Al Geiberger*
Professional Golfer

Athletes have traditionally used psychology to develop an edge or to intimidate their opponents before and during sporting contests. The 1958 New York Yankee baseball team had a relief pitcher named Ryne Duren. Duren, in an attempt to intimidate the batter, intentionally threw his first warm-up pitch over the catcher's head and into the box seats. If you wonder why this intimidated the batter, you need to know something else about Duren: he wore glasses that looked like the cut-off bottoms of milk bottles. There stood a pitcher who looked like he couldn't see throwing wild pitches all over the place. Imagine yourself as a batter waiting to be thrown to (or should I say thrown at) by a pitcher who looked like a blind wild man throwing the ball faster than the speed limit. Could you put your full concentration into hitting the ball? Or, would you direct some attention toward preparing to jump out of the batter's box?

Former heavyweight boxing champion Muhammad Ali, before his 1964 title fight with Sonny Liston, rattled Liston's cage by driving a bus onto the lawn of Liston's Denver home at two o'clock in the morning. After continuously blowing the horn—we don't know whether it was the bus or the horn that woke up Liston— Ali challenged Liston to fight on the lawn. Several episodes of Ali's style of teasing, his poetry, and his dancing in the ring left Liston totally dismayed.

Do you remember the Leonard-Duran fight for the championship title in 1981? Sugar Ray Leonard kept laughing at and teasing Roberto Duran during the first seven rounds. Finally, in the eighth round, Duran was so humiliated that he threw up his hands and quit.

These examples illustrate the psych-out that athletes have used to gain an advantage over their opponents. In these examples, athletes used psychology to undermine their competitors' performance. Can you remember times when you used psychology while playing sports? During a round of golf, have you ever tried to psyche out your opponent by saying something like, "Did you see how well Charlie (your partner) was putting on the practice green? He couldn't miss! There's no stopping him today!" Perhaps your opponents, realizing the game that you were playing, replied "Anyone can putt well on the practice green. I've seen him miss one-footers." Although this kind of scenario has been used by both amateur and professional athletes, the trend is for elite athletes to use psychology to enhance their *own* performance rather than to undermine their opponent's performance, as the following examples will illustrate.

When Sugar Ray Leonard fought Marvelous Marvin Hagler, sports experts had little doubt that both men were in top physical condition. In fact, Hagler appeared to be slightly better prepared. Leonard, however, didn't spar with anyone but chose to use daily mental exercises in which he "visualized" himself fighting and defeating Hagler. Well, Leonard won. I was impressed with his mental training program.

Jack Nicklaus, golf's living legend, always talks about "visualizing" a shot before shooting. Nicholas visualizes every golf shot when standing behind the ball. He visualizes the ball taking off rom the tee, the path that the ball will take during flight, and where the ball will land.

The scope of sport psychology is increasing. *Time* magazine reported that the Canadian figure skating team, to prepare for the most recent Olympics, rented Toronto's Maple Leaf Gardens and simulated Olympic conditions. The Canadian team hired the actual announcer who would be in Calgary and practiced the conditions they anticipated would occur during actual competition. These conditions included a recording of stadium fans shouting and clapping. Why did they do this? To experience the competition before the actual event as a way of familiarizing the thoughts and feelings they would have during competition.

PEAK PERFORMANCE

What is a peak performance?

By peak performances I mean those magic moments when it all comes together—physically, mentally, and emotionally. Such moments are the convergence of the efforts of your mind and your body. The performance appears to exceed ordinary levels of play and results in an achievement of excellence—a personal-best performance.

Can we expect to achieve peak performance every time we play? First the bad news. The answer, of course, is no. Peak performance means reaching the maximum, a high point in performance. By definition, you cannot play your absolute best golf every time you get on a golf course.

The good news is that by understanding the fact that you cannot *peak* every time you play, you can play your best for that day. This philosophy can effectively reduce the pressure you put on yourself always to play at your maximum. Then you can spend your time having fun.

Even if you cannot play at your peak every day, you can increase your level of play in the direction of your peak of performance rather than in the direction of your *valley of performance* by following some simple guidelines. You were exposed to some of these guidelines in previous chapters. In this chapter I will integrate some of the skills you have already learned with some new information. This will allow your golf game to reach a higher level.

How does peak performance feel?

Take a moment to remember a time when you played golf and felt that you couldn't do anything wrong. You drove the golf ball straight down the fairway. You hit your irons to the green as if you were an artist painting a picture. You sent your putts to the middle of the cup. What thoughts did you have during that round of golf? Write down a few of your most important thoughts and feelings.

_____

_____

_____

_____

I can remember my best round of golf ever. I couldn't hear any noise or talking. I had tunnel vision from the ball to my target. I knew that the ball would go where I envisioned. I remember that my swing was slow and smooth. I remember

185

that my swing thought was, "pick it [the golf ball] off the grass." Everything was happening automatically. I hit three flagsticks that day and chipped two in the hole.

What are the psychological characteristics of a peak performance?
According to the pros, golf is 85 percent (Nancy Lopez) to 90 percent (Jack Nicklaus) mental. The higher the skill level of the individual, the more important the mental aspect of the game is. *Mental skills often separate the winner from the loser in a competition in which both athletes are physically equal.* However, neither physical conditioning nor mental conditioning alone will produce a winner; peak performance is a product of the efforts of both mind and body.

   Charles Garfield, author of *Peak Performance: Mental Training Techniques of the World's Greatest Athletes,* identified eight mental and physical conditions that athletes described as representing the feeling that they had at moments when they were performing extraordinarily well. These conditions are

❑ Mentally relaxed. The athletes had a sense of inner calm. They felt they were performing in slow motion with a high degree of concentration.

❑ Physically relaxed. Athletes described feeling that their muscles were loose and fluid.

❑ Confident/optimistic. Each performer had a positive mental attitude and was optimistic about his or her performance.

❑ Focused on the present. Athletes were focused on their performance in the "here and now" (the process) rather on the future (outcome) of the game or on past mistakes.

❑ Highly energized. They had a feeling of high intensity and being "charged."

❑ Extraordinary awareness. The athletes were aware of their own bodies as well as the surrounding athletes.

❑ In control. Everything happened as it should, automatically, without forcing it to happen. Let it happen, rather than make it happen.

❑ In the cocoon. Athletes described a feeling of being completely detached from the external environment and any potential distractions.

DEVELOPING AWARENESS
In each of the conditions described above, the athletes were in tune with their own bodies. These athletes were "active" players. This active role in athletics is similar to active listening during a conversation. I'm sure that you have experienced what

I am about to describe. In a conversation, a person could be a "passive" or an "active" listener. Passive listeners are busy thinking about what they are going to say next. They rarely listen to what the other person is saying. As a result, they are not able to continue the natural flow of conversation based on what the speaker said.

Active listeners, on the other hand, hear what the speaker said and react to the information given. As an active player you are aware of what is happening in your body as well as in your environment. This awareness puts you in control of the situation. To increase the feeling of control, you need to increase your awareness.

1. What should you be aware of? In golf, you should be aware of your emotional state—your state of arousal—and of your environment. Since you have no control over other players or course conditions, your can focus your environmental awareness on the lie of your golf ball, the wind, target conditions, club selection, and so forth.

    The one thing that you do have control over is your arousal level. You know when you are appropriately enthusiastic. You know when you are too excited. Once you become aware of your arousal level, you can adjust it as needed to reach your optimal arousal level for maximum performance. More on this in the next chapter. Each of us has an ideal performance state in which we play our best. This ideal performance state is at a level of arousal that allows us to react to the situation at hand. A PGA Tour player will often come from behind by making a few birdies. He will then get excited, and the adrenalin will start to flow. Before you know it, he is hitting the golf ball over the green. This is fine if he is on 14 or 15. If this surge of energy comes too early, say at 7 or 8, he may begin to make mistakes: it is difficult to play your best when you are over-aroused.

2. The importance of awareness. An active player is aware of his or her strengths and weaknesses. You can use this awareness to maximize your strengths and correct your weaknesses. Put yourself in a position in which you use your strengths and correct your weaknesses. This way you have the advantage. For example, let's say that you always fade your 3 iron and you are in a situation that calls for a 3 iron. Use this shot pattern to help you get to the green. In this case, the active player will play his ball from left-to-right. The passive player will aim for the flag and hope that he hits a straight shot.

DEVELOPING CONFIDENCE

> "One important key to success is self-confidence. An important key to self-confidence is preparation. Complete mental and physical preparation has to do with sacrifice and self-discipline. And that comes from within. Start by setting modest goals which are meaningful, but attainable. For example, every Sunday night write down four things that you want to accomplish for the following week, and then make sure that seven days later when you make up your next list, all four items have been crossed off. These small but meaningful completed tasks should generate much self-confidence as time goes by."
>
> — *Arthur Ashe, Jr.*
> Professional Tennis Player

Confidence is the belief that you can do something. Not only that you can do it but that you can do it correctly time after time. Having confidence invariably produces success. Confident golfers characteristically have positive thoughts, positive self-talk, positive images, and positive dreams. They focus on how to accomplish a task rather than seeing only the barriers in their way. Confident golfers consistently visualize themselves as winning and being successful. The key is that they have enabling thoughts rather than disabling thoughts.

As you learned in Skull Practice, chapter 2, the way you think about yourself reflects your self-confidence and ultimately your behavior. You are only able to do what you tell yourself you can do. You can make positive statements, or affirmations, that promote accomplishing a task (Skull Practice, chapter 4). Affirmations can be used to increase your success rate. Examples of such affirmations are, "When the going gets tough, I get more persistent," "I can do it!" "I will put my golf ball close to the pin," " I really solve problems well," and "Hit it firm."

The confidence-performance relationship
As your confidence increases, your performance increases to an optimal point. Beyond this point, confidence in excess of your skill level will sabotage your performance. The following chart graphically describes this relationship:

THE CONFIDENCE-PERFORMANCE CURVE

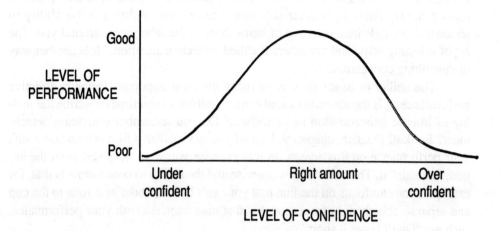

Building confidence

❑ Have a plan. The best way to build confidence is to have a plan for learning, a plan for practice, and a plan for playing. You must stick to your plans. If you learn the correct way to play golf, you will always have a set of sound fundamentals to fall back on, fundamentals that provide you with the assurance that you know what to do in most situations. If your game starts to fall apart, you know where to go to put it back on track. If you know what to do, you increase your confidence that you can do it.

   Practicing correctly will give you the knowledge that you can repeat a specific shot. You can build on this knowledge and draw from the shots you know you can execute when you are faced with a difficult decision on the course.

   Active playing will give you feedback to build a historical foundation. You may think to yourself, "I remember being in this situation before, and that time I _____." Put all these things together and you can figure out what to do in almost any situation.

❑ Be in good physical condition (chapters 9 and 10). Knowing you are fit will improve your confidence. You will know you have the endurance to last through the entire round of golf without getting tired.

❑ Establish a pre-round routine (chapter 1). Establishing a pre-round routine will reduce stress and anxiety about playing golf. A pre-round routine will also help you to concentrate on your game.

What is concentration?

Concentration is the ability to focus your attention on a single item or on a group of related items. There is another side to concentration, and that is the ability to separate that single item or group of items from all the other items around you. The act of selecting some and not others is called "selective attention." It is another way of describing concentration.

The ability to concentrate is probably the most important factor in effective performance. It is the ultimate mental control. Athletes sometimes describe the feeling of intense concentration as "detached." Do you remember practicing detachment? In Skull Practice, chapter 9, I asked you to visualize a film screen and watch your performance on this screen. In this exercise you were detached from the action, "outside" it. The value of this exercise and the ability to concentrate is that, for example, you can focus on the line that your golf ball will take as it rolls to the cup and separate this thought from thoughts that may interfere with your performance, such as, "Don't leave it short."

Concentrating is easy. You can learn and practice this mental skill like any other. But remember, you cannot force concentration. You must let it happen. The more you think about concentration, the less able you are to concentrate.

❑ Attention. Attention is the process of observing yourself and the world around you. Your attention may be internal or external. There are times when an internal focus is appropriate and times when an external focus is appropriate.

An *internal focus* is appropriate when you need to assess your level of arousal. An internal focus could identify your heart beat or breathing rate, the amount of tension in your muscles, or any anxiety that you may have. Focusing internally helps in preparing for a round of golf, in getting ready to execute a golf shot, or in practicing individual components of your golf swing on the practice range.

An *external focus* is appropriate when you need to assess the lie of your ball, the distance you want to carry the ball, the conditions of your target area, or the wind. An external focus is suitable in preparing for a golf shot and essential for the actual execution of the golf shot.

❑ Variation in concentration. A typical round of golf may take about four hours. During this period you need not concentrate the entire time. You need to concentrate for the few seconds that you evaluate the course conditions, select your club, prepare to execute your golf shot. The rest of the time you can relax. Of course, different golfers approach concentration differently. Jack Nicklaus maintains intense concentration throughout a round of golf. He appears detached or indifferent. Lee Trevino, on the other hand, can shift to intense concentration during preparation and execution and then shift his focus back to the crowd. You may have to experiment to see which works best for you.

❑ Mental errors. Mental errors are generally caused by a decline in the intensity of concentration. This decline in concentration can be caused by many factors such as a lack of motivation, fatigue, or distress over something significant in your life such as family, finances, or illness. When you experience a loss of concentration, you begin to make errors in assessing course conditions and in preparing or executing your golf shot. You may tend to push too hard or you may play too fast. Either of these will cause a decline in your performance.

Attention control training

Because of the importance of concentration, I think that you should learn as much as you can to improve your concentration. The following principles will help you to understand more about attention. Several exercises in the last part of this chapter will help you to learn and practice concentration.

❑ Everyone can learn to concentrate. It is a natural process. Golfers need to learn both internal and external kinds of attention.

❑ Golfers need to be able to shift from one kind of attention to the other as the situation requires.

❑ As physiological arousal increases beyond optimal levels, you may tend to pay more attention to how you feel and on specific thoughts (internal focus) rather than assessing your environment and what needs to be accomplished (external focus). Choking occurs as this physiological arousal continues to increase, causing an involuntary narrowing of concentration. This narrowing of concentration causes your attention to become more internal and causes muscular tension.

❑ You can gain control of your ability to concentrate by
    1) Performing a relaxation exercise such as deep breathing.
    2) Altering your focus of attention.
    3) Focusing on the "process" rather than the "outcome."

Paying attention to the process means that you focus on the performance. For example, you might think about the rhythm of your stroke or the ball flight pattern. You want to avoid outcome thinking such as, "If I make this putt, I'll be two strokes ahead and win the tournament" or "If I can reach the green with this shot, I could make an eagle."

191

WHAT GAME ARE THEY PLAYING?

Because you are on a golf course hitting a golf ball with a golf club, can you assume you are playing golf? Most of the time you can. However, there may be more than one game going on at the same time. There is golf and there is mental gymnastics, a game many of us don't know at all. The mental gymnastics game is sometimes started by us and sometimes initiated by someone else in the foursome—usually one of your opponents. Let's take a look at some of these games within the game.

❏ The doubt game. In this game you doubt your ability to play well, or you aren't sure how to get out of the trouble in which you find yourself. This can stem from your lack of sound golf fundamentals or from something someone said. The solution is simple: you need to know good fundamentals and to know that you know. If someone else attempts to shake your confidence, recognize the game that he or she is playing and dismiss it.

❏ The fear game. In this game you are afraid that you will screw up the next shot or your round or your putt. Perhaps you are afraid you will look foolish and everyone will think that you can't play well. Maybe you are worried that you will lose a few dollars on the match. Face your fear directly and shrink it down to size.

❏ Impress-the-others game. You want everyone to think that you can hit the golf ball a mile, or you can get out of the fairway sand bunker and land the ball on the green, or you can sink the 40-foot putt. The other side of this coin is when somone else challenges you to exceed your limit. You can resolve this by knowing your limitations and playing within yourself.

❏ The confidence game. This is another mental game but probably not what you think. It is the other kind of confidence game. It is the player whose behavior sabotages your game. He drops his club on your backswing, she walks on your line, he deliberately goes out of turn, she brings up the rules of the game, and so forth.

The most irritating example of this kind of game is the one in which your opponent lies about his or her handicap in order to get strokes from you, then sets out to beat you as badly as he or she can. This happened to me once. A friend of mine and I met two acquaintances of his. On the first tee, our "opponents" began the chatter about waging a bet and getting strokes. This dialogue is usually fun and part of the excitement of the contest. Finally one of the other men declared that his handicap was 18 and asked for a stroke per hole. I responded that even if his handicap were 18, he shouldn't get a stroke on the par 3s. Watching his practice swing and the way he held the club, there was some doubt in my mind as to his truthfulness.

He turned out to be a good golfer. His putting was super. Without strokes, he made par on the first three holes, then two bogies (which were a net par), then a birdie. We were down six holes. Although I avoid using my sports psychology training to trip someone up, I decided to make an exception. I noticed that putting was the strongest part of his game. So I complimented him on his putting and asked him, "What do you think about when you putt?" Needless to say, he didn't make another putt that day.

Dealing with the confidence game is best handled by prevention: set up the rules before play. If someone is talking around the first tee, state your preferences. Be sure that your behavior is appropriate as well. With the handicap issue, I now volunteer my card so that the others are compelled to follow suit.

❑ The instruction game. The other golfer either asks you for instruction or gives you instruction. This is pretty easy to deal with. Simply state that you neither give nor accept instruction as a matter of policy.

SKULL PRACTICE: LEARNING THE MENTAL SKILLS—BODY SCAN: INSTANT RELAXATION

A body scan is a process in which you focus your attention on various parts of your body to identify any muscular tension. You practiced this exercise in chapter 7. In this section you will refine your technique to achieve instant relaxation. *You do not have to dictate this text into your tape recorder.* Repeat this exercise until you can identify those areas where you hold tension. Soon, you will be able to perform a body scan within seconds and concentrate on those areas that are tense.

1. In a standing position, make yourself comfortable.

2. Take a deep breath and exhale. During the breath, pay attention to the following areas and release all the tension in these areas.

> Pay attention to your *facial muscles*—your eyes, lips, jaw, tongue.
> Identify any areas of tension.
> Release this tension.
>
> Pay attention to your *neck* and *shoulders*.
> Identify any areas of tension.
> Roll your head in a circle and release all tension during the roll.
> Pay attention to your *back*.
> Identify any areas of tension.
> Release all tension.

Pay attention to your *legs*.
Identify any areas of tension.
Release all tension.

Pay attention to your *arms*.
Identify any areas of tension.
Release all tension.

INTEGRATION EXERCISES—GETTING YOUR MIND AND BODY TO WORK AS A UNIT

Exercises to improve concentration

Awareness exercise. Sit in a comfortable place and close your eyes. Pay attention to your breathing. Listen to yourself breathe. Listen to the rhythm of your breathing. If a thought enters your mind, accept it and let it pass through and go back to the rhythm of your breathing. It is impossible to stop thoughts from entering your mind, but it is quite possible to let them pass through without disrupting your concentration. If a negative thought enters your mind or if you think of something upsetting, let the thought pass through your mind and then refocus your attention on your breathing. Do this exercise a couple of times a day.

External focus switch. Sit comfortably and do the following several times, taking about 30 seconds for each. Take a couple of deep breaths and relax. Focus your attention on the sounds you hear. Now focus your attention on what you smell. Now focus on the temperature of the air around you. Focus on the temperature of your own body. If any thoughts enter your mind, disregard them and let them pass through. Listen to the sounds again and repeat the process.

Internal focus switch. Sit comfortably and do the following several times, taking about 30 seconds for each. Take a couple of deep breaths and relax. Pay attention to your breathing. Pay attention to your heart beat. Focus on your hands and your feet. Are they relaxed? Are they warm? Pay attention to your heart again. Focus on your breathing. Focus on the different parts of your body. Dismiss any thoughts that come into your mind. Repeat the process.

Geometrical image. Sit comfortably and close your eyes. Take a couple of deep breaths and relax. Picture a black velvet screen about four feet by five feet. Visualize a magnified golf ball in the middle of the screen. Notice the dimples of the ball. Look at the indentations. Look at the curvature of the design. Notice the writing on the golf ball. Notice the letters. Notice the number.

Using more of your senses. Sit comfortably and close your eyes. Take a couple of deep breaths and relax. Visualize the large black velvet screen again. This time I want you to see a very large lemon. This lemon almost fills the screen. Look at the dimples on the lemon. See the bright yellow color. Notice how the lemon smells. Now take a knife and cut the lemon. Notice how the smell increased. Notice how strong the lemon smells. Cut a wedge of the lemon and take a bite. Notice how tart the lemon tastes. Notice how your eyes and face contract. Repeat this exercise for an orange.

Zoom exercise. Sit in a chair opposite a wall that has nothing on it but an electrical outlet. Take a couple of deep breaths and relax. Notice the entire wall and everything that you can see from the left side to the right side, from the top to the bottom. Take a look at the electrical outlet and notice its shape. Concentrate on the outlet and dismiss all other sights around you. Notice the sockets. Each has three holes. Now notice the entire electrical outlet again. Focus on the entire wall again. Listen to any sounds. Focus on the outlet again. Listen again to the sounds. After you do this exercise a few times, you will see how easy it is to change your focus of attention.

Exercises to improve your awareness of performance
Performance log. If you want to improve your score, you need to identify the areas in your golf game that can use some improvement. To do this you need to be aware of your game. How many fairways do you hit from the tee? How many greens do you reach in regulation? How many greens do you two-putt? What do you do when you get in trouble?

There are many methods for becoming aware of your performance. You can purchase golf logs on which to record your performance, or you can simply use your score card as I do and write the following codes on the line below your score:

a. Upper left corner. Place a check mark if you hit the fairway from the tee. Place two check marks if you are in the fairway with your drive and second shot on a par 5. Place a "G" if you are on the green on a par 3.

b. Upper right corner. Mark whether you made the green in regulation. Use this system:

❑ If you make the green in regulation, put an "R".

❑ If you are there in less than regulation, put a minus sign.

❑ If you are there in more than regulation, put a plus sign.

❑ If you were short on your approach shot, put a down arrow.

❑ If you were long on your approach shot, put an up arrow.

❑ Mark if you were left or right with side arrows.

c. Lower right corner. Indicate your putting success. Use an arrow to indicate if your first put was short, long, right, or left, and a number to indicate how many putts you took.

d. Lower left corner. Indicate trouble—out-of-bounds with an "OB," water with a "W," and trees with a "T."

Analysis of performance. After two or three rounds of golf, you will be able to identify the areas causing you to lose strokes. Once you identify them go to the chapter that discusses that subject and read and practice the exercises. If you believe you need help with the mechanics, make an appointment with your club pro to take a lesson.

Score card description:
Use this system in each block on your score card. If there isn't enough room on your scorecard, make up your own card for analysis purposes.

HOLE	1	2	3	4	5	6	7	8	9	TOTAL OUT
PAR	4	4	3	5	4	5	3	4	4	OUT
	4	5	3	5	6	6	2	3	5	39

Hole 1 Drive in fairway
         On green in regulation
         Putt was on line but short

Hole 2 Drive and second fairway
         Putt was long and right

Hole 3 Drive in fairway
         On green in regulation
         Putt was on line but short

Hole 4   Drive and second was in fairway
On green in regulation
Putt was on line but short

Hole 5   Drive was not in fairway
Green was not reached in regulation
Putt was on line but long

Hole 6   Drive was not in fairway
Green was not reached in regulation
Putt was short and to the right

Hole 7   Drive was on the green
Putt was in

Hole 8   Drive was in fairway
Green was reached in regulation
Putt went in

Hole 9   Drive was not in fairway
Green was not reached in regulation
Putt was long and to the right

CHAPTER 12:

STRESS MANAGEMENT: GETTING

OUT OF YOUR OWN WAY

"The pressure makes me more intent about each shot.
Pressure on the last few holes makes me play better."

— *Nancy Lopez*
Professional Golfer

"I try to make pressure and tension work for me. I
want the adrenalin to be flowing. I think sometimes
we try so hard to be cool, calm, and collected that we
forget what we're doing. There's nothing wrong with
being charged up if it's controlled."

— *Hale Irwin*
Professional Golfer

When I conduct stress management workshops, I ask each participant to tell the class his or her name and reason for taking the class. My purpose is to allow the participants to become comfortable with each other and for me to determine the topics I need to focus on. During one of my workshops a man about sixty years old stated his name and his reason for attending the workshop: "I've had high blood pressure all my life and I recently had quadruple bypass surgery. My doctor told me to come."

Later in the workshop I was discussing the relationship between our reaction to an event and the amount of stress we feel from that event. I used this example: I was driving in the middle lane of a six-lane city street when someone entered the roadway from the right and cut in front of me to the left lane. I told the class that I could have reacted by blowing the horn, shaking my fist, riding his tail, or making a gesture to let him know how displeased I was with his behavior. I also had another option: back off and watch the drama of life unfold in front of me. I told the class that in situations like this I choose the last option—I back off and let the driver slip through.

Immediately the heart patient jumped in and asked me, "Doesn't that make you mad?" I replied, "No, I prefer to back off and let the driver through." The patient said, "It makes me mad. I can't see how you can let him go without doing something." As I looked at the guy, I saw that his eyes were protruding, his face was red, and he was sitting at the edge of the chair. I asked him, "How do you feel right now?" He told me that he felt excited, hot, sweaty, and tense, and his heart was beating fast. I asked him if this was the way he usually felt when he got mad, and he told me that it was. I began to see why he had high blood pressure all his life and had to have bypass surgery. He reacted to the situation that I described as if as if it were actually happening to him. The problem with stress is that you may react to every insignificant situation as if it were life-threatening. Unless this heart patient changed his attitude, he was clearly destined to have more health problems. I agree, there are times when you need to stand your ground, but the situation I described is not one of them. This patient didn't understand that a conscious decision to allow the driver to get through *was* "doing something." It was an "in charge" decision, a decision that kept me in control rather than giving up control to the other driver.

If you are prone to stress, you are prone to tension and anxiety. Tension and anxiety prevent you from performing your best. If you want to play your best, you need to manage stress both on and off the golf course.

EXCITEMENT AND PERFORMANCE

When we think about participating in sports, words such as arouse, activate, charge, electrify, kindle, fire, stimulate, and spark come into our minds. Playing a sport is exciting and invigorating. The more excited we are, the more energy we have and the better we play. Up to a point that is. Beyond that point any additional excitement usually interferes with performance. This point is different for different sports, as you shall see. High stress usually produces arousal, but at a higher level than that which promotes peak performance. Let's look at the arousal-performance relationship first, and then we'll look at the relationship between stress and performance.

THE AROUSAL-PERFORMANCE RELATIONSHIP

In golf, you don't have control over the other players and you don't have control over course conditions. You do, however, have control over yourself. You have control over your diet, your state of physical fitness, your equipment, your mental attitude, your perspective, and your arousal level. In previous chapters I have discussed each of these factors except equipment, which is not within the scope of this book. If you performed the exercises in the mental skills sections, you now know how to relax. Knowing how to relax will allow you to control your arousal levels. Your ability to relax and control your thoughts are the keys.

What is sports arousal?

Arousal is an energizing function of our bodies that releases our resources for activity. When we sense danger or need energy, this energizing function kicks in. Our hypothalamus—the part of our brain that controls arousal—sends out signals to the various parts of our bodies in charge of arousal, resulting in increased heart rate and increased blood pressure, a redistribution of blood from our digestive system and extremities to the large muscles, and a release of adrenalin from our adrenal glands, located above our kidneys. Our blood sugar and breathing rate also increase.

We are able to exercise some control over our arousal. Driving a car in New York City may stimulate the "fight or flight" response in the best of us, especially if we get caught up in the near-panic of activity. It's possible, though, to take a deep breath, relax, sit back, and enjoy the drama—a valuable skill to master for those times when you are going to attempt a ten-foot birdie putt for the club championship. But there are times when you need to get energized. When a weight lifter is going to do a lift and jerk, he may want to create as much arousal as possible to put forward his best effort. You need to have a low level of arousal to play well. Moreover, during your tee shot you may want to be a little more aroused than when you are putting.

What should you know about arousal? First, that there is a wide range of arousal states, second, that each situation or sport may require a different level of arousal, and third, that you need to assess and adjust your level of arousal to match the arousal needs of a specific situation. You have the ability to control your arousal; you just have to learn how.

What is the relationship between arousal and performance?

A certain amount of arousal is necessary for all activity. All other factors being equal, optimal arousal means optimal performance. Too much arousal or too little arousal usually causes a decline in performance.

The decline in performance is demonstrated in the performance curve on the following page.

The performance curve illustrates that as arousal increases from drowsy to alert, there is a progressive *improvement* in performance. Once arousal increases beyond the alert state to a state of high excitement, there is a corresponding *decline* in performance. This information is important to know because if you are able to match your level of arousal with the demands of your golf situation, you will perform better.

THE AROUSAL-PERFORMANCE CURVE

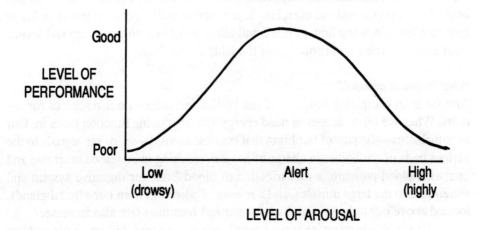

What are the effects of over-arousal?

The problem most of us have is not that we don't get excited but that we get too excited. Over-excitement causes a decline in motor coordination, a narrowed field of vision, an improper focus of attention, and a decline in concentration—an impairment, that is, of all the factors necessary for optimal performance. You may perceive the demands of your golf game to exceed your resources to meet those demands. Fear, worry, anxiety, and panic will reduce your confidence.

Assessing your own level of arousal

An increase in the level of arousal produces both psychological and physiological changes. Look for these factors: fear, anxiety, a decline in self-confidence or concentration, and an increase in heart rate, blood pressure, or respiration.

If you want to assess your arousal, ask yourself these questions just prior to play: (circle your response):

	OVER-AROUSAL	IN CONTROL
1. Is my heart racing?	yes	no
2. Are my thoughts rushing?	yes	no
3. Are my palms sweaty?	yes	no
4. Am I able to concentrate?	no	yes
5. Do I have confidence?	no	yes
6. Am I afraid?	yes	no
7. Do I feel tense and pressured?	yes	no

202

How to adjust arousal

All athletes must constantly monitor and adjust their arousal levels. Golf requires problem-solving, decision-making, and fine motor coordination, all of which are best achieved at low-to-moderate arousal. You need to identify your arousal level and adjust it when it is not within acceptable range. This adjustment can be accomplished through one or more of the following techniques, discussed in the SKULL PRACTICE sections of the previous chapters.

- ❑ Listen to your thoughts. Are they psyching you up or psyching you out?
- ❑ Breathing. Focus on a regular, relaxed breathing rhythm. To energize, inhale energy, exhale fatigue. To relax, exhale tension.
- ❑ Use imagery. To energize, take a deep breath and imagine an energy machine, such as a steam engine. To relax, go to your mental room.
- ❑ Take energy from spectators or disassociate from the pace of those around you, if they are going too fast.
- ❑ Remove or resolve unnecessary sources of energy drain such as memories of emotional conflicts.
- ❑ Distract yourself from fatigue or excitement by concentrating on the process of getting your ball from point A to point B.

Match your arousal level with your golf situation

Ideally, you can be physiologically and psychologically ready to perform without tension or over-arousal. Relaxation is an adjustment of arousal toward a calm, confident, and restful state.

Of course, the best plan to avoid over excitement during play is prevention. Approach the competition several days in advance and develop a pace that keeps your arousal low. You can help yourself by practicing relaxation exercises daily.

Remember, if your level of arousal is beyond optimal, you will want to perform your breathing and body scan exercises to help yourself relax.

STRESS AND PERFORMANCE

High levels of stress produce excess arousal. Excess arousal interferes with performance. So if you want to perform at your highest level, you need to manage stress. To do that, you need to understand it, what it is, how it affects you, when you are being affected, and how to deal with it. Let's start from the beginning.

What is stress?

Stress is the nonspecific response of the body to any demand made upon it.

Demands can be biological (injury, illness, diet, puberty), psychological (self-esteem, thoughts, perceptions, anxiety, coping skills), social (relationship with family, friends, coworkers), behavioral (time management, procrastination, exercise), or environmental (noise, wind, rain). The experience can be pleasant (marriage, vacation, promotion) or unpleasant (death of loved one, injury, illness, losing job). An additional constituent, a combination of psychological and behavioral factors, is how the individual perceives the event. What may be viewed as stressful by one person may not be viewed as stressful by someone else.

Our ability to handle stress depends on our coping resources, which are related to our personalities, anxiety levels, self-esteem, fears, locus of control, and personal needs. Coping resources are improved by good friends or family, and may reduce stress.

What causes stress?

Some psychologists believe that the major events in your life are the most important cause of stress. These events include the death of a spouse (#1), divorce (#2), marriage, vacation, loss of a job, moving to a new city, illness, and bankruptcy. Marriage and vacation are positive events but are nevertheless considered stressful events.

Other psychologists believe that daily hassles contribute more to stress than major life events. Getting the children to day-care on time, preparing dinner, driving to work in traffic, and balancing the check book add up to a lot of tension.

Our vulnerability to stress also counts. Factors relating to our vulnerability are gender, age, role, locus of control, self-esteem, learned helplessness, need levels, anxiety, tolerance of ambiguity, and coping skills.

The significance of the stress response

You read earlier that to maximize your golf performance it is important to regulate your arousal, because over-arousal can produce a decline in performance; stay relaxed, because increased muscular tension produces a decline in performance; and maintain awareness, because awareness keeps you in control. You need to be aware of what is happening inside to be able to sense when adjustments are necessary.

The stress response interferes with each of these important factors by causing your arousal levels to go out of control. Stress produces muscular tension, which tightens your muscles and prevents them from generating maximum clubhead speed. It alters your focus of attention and prevents you from maintaining awareness.

Increasing your awareness

How do you know when you are under stress? Here are several easy-to-identify signs of stress.

❑ Rapid heart rate.

❑ Dryness of the throat and mouth.

❑ Feelings of weakness or dizziness.

❑ Inability to concentrate.

❑ Floating anxiety.

❑ Muscular Tension.

❑ Excess sweating.

❑ Indigestion or upset stomach.

DEALING WITH STRESS

Much of what you have learned in the previous chapters has taught you how to deal with stress. You learned how to manage your time by planing your work, practice, and play schedule. You learned about self-esteem and how believing in yourself will help you to make better decisions. You learned how to set goals and plan your improvement, how to identify your internal dialogue and how to change your thoughts when necessary. You have also practiced relaxation exercises that taught you how to breathe, how to relax, how to visualize, and how to create pictures in your mind that would remove anxiety about each golf shot.

Robert Elliott, MD in his book *Is it Worth Dying For?* summed it up pretty nicely when he said: "Don't sweat the small stuff. And remember, it's all small stuff."

The following are some suggestions for dealing with stress:

❑ Express yourself. Express your thoughts and feelings. Learning how to be assertive, expressing your feelings, and learning from past experiences can help.

❑ Think positive. Develop a realistic, positive attitude. Be alert to traps such as "I have to," "I must," and "If only."

❑ Learn to unwind. Listen to music, exercise, meditate, or go out and have some fun.

❑ Eat right. Eat a balanced diet with plenty of whole grains, fruit, and vegetables. Avoid coffee, refined sugar, and junk food.

❑ Manage your time. Avoid feeling rushed.

❑ Start an exercise program. Exercise, such as swimming, running, brisk walking, and biking is a very good stress manager.

SKULL PRACTICE: LEARNING THE MENTAL SKILLS

> One time Tommy Bolt (professional golfer), known
> for his graceful swing and terrible temper, was trying
> to enliven a clinic, he asked his fourteen-year-old son
> to "show the nice folks what I taught you." The son
> obediently hurled a nine-iron into the blue sky.*

Managing your emotions

Emotions are feelings. They are neither good nor bad. It is how we express them or don't express them that makes them positive or negative.

Emotions affect our attitude, our approach to solving problems, and our personalities. Positive emotions can elevate our mood and increase our enthusiasm. They can initiate a positive mental attitude that, in turn, can pave the way to improved performance. They can open a lot of doors to help you solve problems, whether these problems are with your golf game or your personal life.

Negative emotions, on the other hand adversely affect your mood, attitude and personalities. They are accompanied by physical changes in our bodies similar to the changes that occur when we are under stress. These changes are detrimental to our performance. When we are experiencing negative emotions, we begin to think negatively, "Don't be short" on an uphill putt instead of, "Hit it firm." Negative emotions also create muscle tension, limiting the extension of our arms and legs and the release of the clubhead through the ball.

How do people react emotionally to adverse conditions on the golf course? Golf professionals often hit their golf balls off the beaten track into a "trouble" situation. It's what they do next that is crucial. The golfer may see this as a challenge or as a disaster. If she sees it as a challenge, she calls up her creative powers to solve the problem. The result of this approach is usually favorable. If the golfer sees the golf shot as a disaster, he loses control and begins to question his ability to repair the damage or even his ability to play well. The negative internal dialogue begins: "This is not my day." "I should have used the 3 wood." "I should have . . ." Soon negative emotions begin to display themselves: fear, frustration, anger, and disgust. This cycle can be short if the golfer has mastered some mental skills.

The best strategy to deal with negative emotions is prevention. You can prevent negative emotions from appearing by having a game plan, a pre-shot routine, good control over your arousal, and good control over your internal dialogue. If you slip, and most of us do, you can focus on your fundamentals and

---

* *Anecdotes*, Fadiman, Little, Brown Publishers, Boston.

plan to make a good solid swing through the ball. You need to focus on what you want to accomplish rather than on what happened or the difficulty of the next shot. You can follow these steps.

❑ Decide that you are in control of your life.

❑ Acknowledge that you own your feelings. No one can "make" you mad. Only you can make yourself mad.

❑ Accept that sometimes you will make mistakes.

❑ Accept that you are not perfect.

❑ Stick to your pace.

❑ Follow your game plan.

❑ Adhere to your pre-shot routine.

❑ Breathe deeply.

❑ Play the percentage shot.

INTEGRATION EXERCISES—GETTING YOUR MIND AND BODY TO WORK AS A UNIT

In reading this book, you have learned a great deal about golf, your mental approach, and you. I have attempted to teach you skills that will help you improve your golf game. Learning those skills is important. Of equal importance is clearing the way for you to use those skills to improve your golf game.

Getting out of your own way

There are times when, even though we know what to do, we unconsciously manipulate a situation so as not to get what we want. This process is called self-sabotage. Take the man who really doesn't want the job for which he is interviewing. He unconsciously withholds information that would make him attractive as an employee. A woman may act as if she doesn't understand mechanical things or math because she thinks the people she is with expect her not to know about these things. Such behavior prevents someone from expressing his true self. It prevents him from getting what he wants. Finding your self-sabotaging behavior is simple. Correcting it is also simple.

A quick test

Take this quick test. If you have more than five checks, you may want to spend time thinking about what you can do to deal with these subjects.

207

_____ 1. My life often seems out of control.

_____ 2. I spend a lot of time on other people's problems.

_____ 3. I often get into trouble by assuming I know something.

_____ 4. I tend to expect the worst.

_____ 5. I often find myself saying, "I don't feel up to it."

_____ 6. The fear of appearing stupid often prevents me from asking
        questions or offering my opinion.

_____ 7. I have trouble receiving criticism, even from family or friends.

_____ 8. If I don't do something perfectly, I feel worthless.

_____ 9. I have trouble focusing on what is really important to me.

_____ 10. I often wish I were someone else.

_____ 11. I often feel irritable and moody.

_____ 13. I waste a lot of time.

_____ 14. I often do not live up to my potential because I put tasks off
        to the last minute.

_____ 15. I spend time with people who belittle me or put down my
        thoughts or ideas.

How we sabotage ourselves

Many of us, through our behavior, limit our likelihood to reach our maximum
potential. Such behaviors are learned and, therefore, can be unlearned. Here is a
summary of some of the important behaviors that can sabotage our lives.

1. Blaming others. A self-defeating habit. We make the other guy the bad
   guy. We blame the boss at work, our spouse at home, or the kids, when
   there is no one else to blame.

   Solution: Take responsibility for your actions.

2. Lack of focus. A problem of not having defined goals. Some people live
   from one problem to the next or spend their time working on other
   people's goals.

   Solution: Write down the three most important goals you have.

3. Not being informed. People make assumptions or base their decisions on hunches, feelings, or impulse without regard for the facts.

   Solution: Keep your focus on the facts, not on interpretations.

4. Hanging out with negative people. Some people surround themselves with people who discourage them and treat them as if they will never amount to much.

   Solution: Evaluate your friends. If they are not supportive, you can always find new friends.

5. Expecting failure. The law of self-fulfilling prophecies states, "If you predict that something will happen, the likelihood of it happening increases."

   Solution: You can set yourself up for success or failure—the choice is yours. You essentially get what you expect.

6. Not learning from others. Successful people have this in common: they are open to new ideas, they ask questions, and they know how to listen.

   Solution: When you have problems, ask someone who knows.

7. Self-defeating thinking patterns. Thinking patterns can make situations worse than they really are. Examples of this are black-and-white thinking, taking things personally—that is, interpreting innocent events as being directed toward you—and disregarding the positive crediting someone else with your achievements.

   Solution: Listen to your thoughts and refute them when they are irrational.

8. Being stopped by failures. Everyone makes mistakes. If you let one failure indicate that *you* are a failure, you can get stuck.

   Solution: Put a mistake or failure in perspective.

SECTION F

APPENDICES

APPENDIX I:

IMPORTANT GOLF TERMS

Address
The process through which the player positions his body and the club for a golf swing or a putting stroke.

Alignment
The arrangement of the parts of the body and the clubface in relation to the target line.

Approach shot
A golf shot made within a distance close enough to reach the green.

Backswing
The motion of the club, hands, arms, and body away from the ball.

Backspin
The backward rotation of the golf ball on its horizontal axis. This rotation is imparted on the golf ball by the golf club and causes the ball to fly high and stop quickly when it lands.

Bump and run
A shot around the green that is played deliberately into a bank or a hill to slow the speed of the ball while letting it move in a forward direction.

Bunker
A sandy or grassy hollow forming an obstacle on the course.

Centrifugal force
The action of a rotating body to move away from the center. The golfer feels this force in the downswing as an extension of the arms as the club travels in a circular path.

213

Chip and run
A low trajectory golf shot played to the green or the apron of the green causing the golf ball to roll farther than its carry (distance in the air).

Closed clubface
The toe of the clubface leads the heel causing the clubface to point to the left of the target line.

Closed stance
The position, at address, in which the line drawn through the toes of the shoes points to the right of the target line.

Cut shot
A golf shot in which the golf ball is struck with a slightly open clubface while the clubhead path is traveling to the left of the target. This produces a clockwise spin on the golf ball which makes the ball travel from left-to-right. This spin also helps the ball to stop quickly on the green.

Deceleration
A slowing down of the golf club during a swing or a stroke prior to hitting the ball. This results in a lower clubhead speed which reduces the distance the ball travels.

Divot
A piece of grass displaced by the golf club. The divot occurs in front of the golf ball when the club is swung properly.

Draw
A golf shot that curves in a right-to-left path.

Dynamic balance
The transfer of weight from the right side to the left side during the golf swing, while maintaining body control.

Fade
A golf shot that curves in a left-to-right path.

Fat shot
A golf shot in which the golf club hits the ground before it hits the golf ball.

Flat swing
A swing that uses a more horizontal plane than normal.

Follow-through
The remainder of the swing after the ball has been struck.

Forward press
Movement of the hands, arms, or leg that signals the beginning of the swing.

Forward swing
(Forward swing)—The motion of the body, arms, hands, and club in the direction of the target.

Fried egg
A lie in the sand where the landing of the ball has splashed the immediate sand away and the ball is deeper in the sand than one-half its height.

Grain
The direction in which the blades of grass grow and lie on the putting surface. Grain usually follows the runoff, sun, mowing cuts, and prevailing wind.

High side
The side of the cup which is highest on a sidehill breaking putt. This is also called the "pro side."

Lever system
The bones of the skeletal system acting in concert to act as levers.

Line
The path on which the golfer intends the ball to travel.

Line of flight
The direction the ball actually travels.

Loft
The degree of pitch built into the clubface.

One-piece-takeaway
The early portion of the backswing in which the arms, hands, and wrists move away from the ball in the same relation to each other as they were at address.

Open clubface
The heel of the club leads the toe of the club causing the clubface to point to the right of the target line.

Open stance
The position, at address, in which the line drawn through the toes of the shoes points to the left of the target line.

Pace
The rate of movement in the swing.

Path
The directional arc in which the club is swung (viewed from the top).

Pendulum stroke
A free swing from a fixed pivot point usually at the center of the chest while the arms and shoulders move-during the putting stroke.

Pinch shot
A short shot around the green struck with a crisp, descending blow.

Pitch-and-run
A short, lofted shot having more than a customary amount of roll after it lands.

Pitch shot
A high trajectory shot of short length, played with one of the more lofted iron clubs such as the 9-iron, pitching wedge, or sand wedge.

Plumb bob
A method of determining the direction that the golf ball will break on the putting surface. It relies on sighting the slope while using the putter as a vertical reference.

Reading the green
The processing of deciding the correct path and pace to roll the golf ball into the hole. Factors to consider include: length of grass, type of grass, grain, firmness of the ground, slope, dryness, wind, the ball, the club, and the technique.

Recover
To play a golf shot from an undesirable ball location to a more desirable location.

Rhythm
A synchronized movement in the swing with a regular and repeating pattern.

Setup
The mechanical procedure through which you position your body and clubface in relation to the ball and target line.

Short game
The part of the game played around the green to include pitching, chipping, sand shots, and putting.

Slice
A ball which curves excessively from left-to-right.

Spot-putting
Using an intermediate target in putting.

Square
A term which refers to having the clubface at right angles to the target line and having the shoulders, hips, knees, and toes parallel to the target line.

Stance
The position of the feet when the player address the ball.

Sweet spot
The point of the clubface which does not allow the club to torque (twist) when you hit the ball.

Swing center
A point around which the circular motion of the arms and upper trunk are made.

Swing plane
An imaginary flat, thin surface which is used to describe the path and angle on which the club is swung.

Target line
An imaginary straight line drawn from behind and through the ball toward the intended target.

Tempo
The rate of the swing.

Three-quarter shot
A shot played with less than the normal length backswing of effort designed to achieve about 70-80% of the regular distance for that club.

217

Timing
The sequencing of the body parts and the club to achieve the most effective and efficient motion.

Touch
A delicate sense of feel, especially in chipping and putting.

Trajectory
The path a ball takes in the air, especially the height and path of the ball.

Visualization
Forming a mental picture of the correct swing, stroke, or desired result prior to swinging the club.

Waggle
A movement made prior to the swing with the purpose of staying relaxed, establishing comfort, or setting pace.

APPENDIX II:

LEARNING METHODS

In the introduction, I discussed various learning styles. The styles that I discussed were: intellectual, visual, and kinesthetic. These styles are a modification of learning theories which are described as visual, auditory, and kinesthetic. Each learning style relates to either the right brain or the left brain. The right side of your brain is creative and the left side is logical. Therefore, exercises that relate to the right side of your brain helps to develop your creativity. Exercises that relate to the left side of your brain develop your reasoning abilities.

Visual learning
Associates with the right side of your brain. If you are a visual learner, you tend to be creative and artsy. Visual learners are usually more concerned with the process than the result and they see things in shades of gray rather than black and white. Visual learners usually prefer to write things down to remember them.

Auditory learning
Associates with the left side of your brain. If you are an auditory learner, you tend to be calculating, judgmental, self- critical, and result oriented. Auditory learners remember things by hearing them.

Kinesthetic learning
Associates with both sides of your brain. Kinesthetic learners learn best by doing. The pitfall in this learning type is that the individual may learn and not understand what it is that they are doing because he or she failed to listen and watch carefully.

WHAT DO YOU NEED TO KNOW ABOUT THESE
LEARNING STYLES?
If you are a visual learner, you learn best by watching someone who has perfected

the technique. Video tapes are an excellent learning tool for you. You can watch the video and freeze-frame to study each specific position. Greg Norman has said he learned golf by watching Jack Nicklaus' tapes.

If you are an auditory learner, you learn best by traditional teaching methods. You can most effectively learn by getting into a group in which the teacher takes you through each step. One-on-one instruction may suit you best or, at most, one-on-five instruction.

If you are an kinesthetic learner, your most efficient method for learning is by a coach moving your arms, legs and body in the correct position to accomplish a skill. You will probably benefit most from individual instruction.

THE BEST METHOD
There is no best method for everyone. As I mentioned in the introduction, you need to evaluate your method of learning and involve yourself in learning environments that capitalize on your method of learning. This does not mean, however, that you forsake the other methods. It means that you should be sure that you include the method that is most compatible with your learning style *and* learn what you can from the other methods.

APPENDIX III:
DEVELOPING A POSITIVE MENTAL
ATTITUDE

AFFIRMATIONS TO HELP YOU DEVELOP HIGH
SELF-ESTEEM AND A POSITIVE MENTAL ATTITUDE

There are days when things just are not going right. No matter what we do, everything seems to be falling apart. We all have these days. What separates the survivors from those who fall on the sidelines is what you do when you are having "one-of-those-days." The following affirmations (positive statements designed to turn around even the worst day of your life).

You may want to select a few of the following statements to be your very own—to use whenever you see fit:

1. I accept myself unconditionally.

2. I like myself.

3. I am a unique person.

4. I have a lot to offer to everyone I meet,

5. I can evaluate situations and determine a good way of dealing with them.

6. I have had many successes in life and will continue to succeed.

7. I always conduct myself at the highest moral and ethical levels.

8. I have an excellent relationship with my family and friends.

9. I always give people who I meet a chance.

10. I always have the option to choose not to spend time with someone who is not compatible with my positive feelings about myself and those I care about.

221

11. I enjoy pursuing my goals.

12. I have great perseverance and tenacity and follow through with my goals.

13. I have the ability to make, define, and keep my commitments.

14. I feel positive and confident.

15. I am in control of my mind and body at all times.

16. I accept only positive thoughts, images, and feelings.

17. My self-worth does not depend on my performance.

18. I don't have to be perfect.

19. I am observant.

20. I am aware.

21. I can concentrate easily.

22. My mind is always on what I am doing.

23. I keep myself in good mental and physical condition.

24. I am able to take a step back and let the drama of life unfold before me.

25. I enjoy being self-motivated.

26. I tune out unfair or inappropriate criticism.

27. I am never intimidated by the thoughts or opinions of others.

28. Whenever anyone tries to "psyche me out," I take a step back and recognize the game that they are playing.

29. I always enjoy a good rapport with fellow players.

30. I have complete immunity to negative comments or thoughts.

31. I always enjoy maintaining emotional control.

32. I accept responsibility for my successes as well as my shortcomings.

33. I always maintain a positive mental attitude even after mistakes or bad breaks.

34. I use bad breaks or mistakes to direct my efforts to excel even more.

35. I always make the right decisions at the time.

36. I enjoy being a creative and resourceful person.

37. I see all situations as learning experiences.

38. I have a great ability to adjust positively to all physical and mental situations.

39. I thoroughly enjoy all aspects of golf.

40. I take pride in practicing good sportsmanship.

41. I am mastering the techniques of golf.

42. I enjoy setting reasonable goals for my golf performance.

43. I enjoy achieving my goals in golf.

44. I am able to turn around any interruption to the flow of play.

45. I enjoy practicing new drills and exercises that can help me to develop my techniques.

46. I never pout when things don't go my way.

47. I reject all thoughts that result in fear.

48. I am able to go to sleep easily and awaken alert and refreshed.

49. I feel physically fit at all times.

50. I possess great reserves of strength and energy and can mobilize them on demand.

APPENDIX IV:

HOW TO FIND A TEACHING PRO

A Conversation with Teaching Pro Jonathan Rinkevich *

GSF When a golfer decides to take lessons, he or she may not know how to locate a teaching professional. How would you suggest finding a teaching pro?

JLR Probably the best method is through friends or golfers you have met. If you know someone who plays well, he or she may be a good resource for you. If you are not able to get 3-4 names from this method, you may want to go to several golf courses, talk to the head pros, and ask them who they would suggest. If you keep hearing the same name over and over again, that is probably the teacher for you.

Ask a lot of questions. Ask about their style of teaching. Ask about which tour players have an ideal swing. Ask if they are happy correcting a problem in your swing or if they prefer to teach someone from scratch. Listen to their answers. The way they answer can tell you more than the answers to your questions.

If you are a beginner, you may want to ask them about their group lessons or clinics. As you advance in ability, individual lessons become more important.

GSF Can you describe an ideal teacher?

JLR An ideal teacher is aware of the student's needs. He or she must have a sixth sense that tells him or he what is right for a student. Teachers have

---

* Jonathan L. Rinkevich is a PGA golf professional at Fred Enke Municipal Golf Course, Tucson, Arizona. He has played golf professionally on the South African Tour and on several United States mini-tours.

225

to be good listeners. For example, I usually ask new students to describe the last three holes of their last round of golf. If they describe playing well except around the green, I know that they need a short game lesson. If they bogied or doubled bogied a hole by getting up and down, I know they need a full swing lesson. Seventy-five percent of the time people need a short game lesson and not a full swing lesson.

An ideal teacher is one who has good communication skills. This means that they listen to what the student says and that they are able to tell students what to do in many different ways. This last point relates to the teacher having many tools in his or her teaching bag.

A good teacher has to have a good command of the modern fundamentals of golf and be able to convey them in an understandable manner to the student. The teacher must be able to demonstrate or show in pictures how the swing should look.

Another important factor is the ability to motivate students to learn and to practice what they have learned. A teacher must make students feel good about themselves, their game, and their potential to improve.

There is a simple method of teaching and that method is this:

a. Tell the student what you are going to say.

b. Say it.

c. Tell them what you told them.

GSF Is there an attitude that students can have that makes them an ideal student?

JLR The ideal student comes into a lesson with an open mind. Ideal students describe how they play golf and what they want to learn from lessons. Some people just want to hit the ball in the air while others want to perfect their swings to lower their handicaps into the single digits.

They ask many questions and are not afraid to be assertive and say, "I don't understand." They are not afraid to say, "I'm having trouble with this. Can we do it a different way." Ideal students have goals and are willing to commit to practice time.

GSF Are there any things that hamper the learning process?

JLR Yes, there are many obstacles to learning. First, there is the problem of matching learning styles. Hopefully, the instructor is able to adapt to the learning style of the student. A second problem is that of the student's personality. Some students, especially the low handicappers, resist learning something new. Other students are afraid that learning a new thing will mess them up permanently.

Another area that may hamper the learning process is the student's expectations—how well you expect to hit the ball, what score you want to make, and so forth. If you want to improve your golf game, in what time frame do you expect to arrive at your goal? This relates to proper goal-setting that you mention in your book. The student's goal must be reasonable and attainable. I can't help to lower someone's handicap from 18 to 5 in only two weeks.

GSF   What is the relative value of individual lessons versus group lessons?

JLR   Group lessons are ideal for beginners. Beginners feel intimidated and need to be around a group of golfers who play at their level. Group lessons are relatively inexpensive. One caution that I have is that the group is not too large for the instructor. The ideal situation is to have 4-5 students per instructor in a one-hour clinic. In this way, each student will receive some individual attention.

  Individual lessons are better for anyone with a handicap of 18 or less. You shouldn't rule out individual lessons for beginners. You can rule out group lessons for anyone with a handicap of 15 or less because students won't get the individual attention that they need.

GSF   What about golf schools?

JLR   Golf schools are group lessons, but on a bigger scale. With golf schools, you need to have a lot of stamina to hit balls for hours at a time. If you get tired after a half-hour to an hour, you may not get the most benefit from a golf school.

GSF   What do you think about a video taped golf lesson?

JLR   This is probably the best thing in the world for learning golf. You can see on the screen exactly what you are doing in your swing—what you are doing correctly and what you are doing incorrectly. If a person is a visual learner, this is the ideal teaching method.

GSF   What about golf instruction video tapes?

JLR   Some instruction video tapes are better than others. The problem with golf instruction video tapes is that they teach you the way the golf pro swings rather than adapting to the way you swing. Instruction video tapes work best with beginners because the student can re-run the tap over and over to learn the grip, the set-up, and other fundamentals.

  A related problem that I sometimes encounter is when a student reads an article in one of the golf magazines stating that so-and-so hits his drives 20 yards longer by doing "this." The student comes to me for a lesson and asks if he can hit the ball longer by doing the same thing. Well, it may work for so-and-so but it may not work for you with your swing.

GSF Can you give some tips on taking a lesson?

JLR I can give some basic suggestions about how to take a lesson.

❑ The student and the instructor should agree on the objective of the lesson.

❑ You should identify how you learn—auditory, visual, or kinesthetic—and relate this information to the instructor.

❑ You should ask questions about anything you don't understand.

❑ You should fully disclose your strengths and shortcomings. For example, if you can only hit you 5 iron 130 years, tell your instructor.

❑ Be open minded and give the lesson a chance.

❑ Don't expect a quick cure. Permanent improvement takes some effort and some time.

❑ Discuss what you learned with your instructor—some instructors will write out what they have taught you that day. Keep a record of your lessons.

GSF How should someone practice?

JLR I can give you a few guidelines for practice on the practice range.

❑ Make practice competitive—set practice goals. For example, sink 7 out of 10 putts from within 8 feet.

❑ Create course situations on the practice range—use a 9 iron to hit to an area on the practice range. Think that the area that you are hitting to is the 18th hole on the last day of an important tournament.

❑ Practice how you play—do everything from your pre-shot routine to your debriefing shot.

❑ Do not practice when you are tired, are in a bad mood, frustrated, or in bad weather.

❑ If you are confident in your mechanics and they are working for you, don't continue to try different things, especially in putting. If its not broken, don't fix it!

❑ Keep a log of your practice sessions:
> What did you want to accomplish?
> How do you intend to accomplish your goals?
> How did the practice session go?

What did you learn during the session?

❑ Vary club selection during practice on the practice range.

GSF Many times people on the course or on the practice range attempt to help someone to correct a problem in their swing. I hear things like, "You picked up your head." or "You're not turning your hands over." Do you want to comment on these situations?

JLR Most people can identify a result [picking up] of something that was done incorrectly as in your example. However, these people have no clue as to what *caused* this result (e.g. breaking your wrists too early allows the club to get ahead of your hands and the result is that you pick up your head).

The best approach to take in a situation like this is to say something like, "I never take instruction while I'm on the course."

GSF People are always talking about "feel." I usually hear this when someone whispers, "I just don't have any feel today." What do you think about feel?

JLR Feel changes all the time. It changes by the minute. It is never constant. Feel changes, but mechanics are constant. For example, your setup is always the same, your position on the top is always the same, the angle of the club to your forearm is always the same. If you go back to the basics and check your grip and stance, you can re-create your feel. Do this and relax and your feel will come back to you. Occasionally, there are days that you just have to accept the fact that you are not going to have the feel that you want.

APPENDIX V:

SUGGESTED READING AND

VIEWING LIST

A. Golf—Fundamentals
Five Lessons: The Modern Fundamentals of Golf, Hogan, B., Fireside, 1985.
Golf Swing, Leadbetter, D. and Juggan, J., Green, 1990.
How to Become a Complete Golfer, Toski, B. and Flick, J., Progolfers, 1984.
Nancy Lopez's the Complete Golfer, Lopez, N. and Wade, T., Contemporary, 1989.
Play Better Golf, Irwin, H., Smith, 1983.
Tempo, Geiberger, A. and Dennis, L., Golf Digest, 1986.

B. Golf—Mental Aspects
Mind Mastery for Winning Golf, Rotella, R. and Bunker, L., P-H, 1986.
Personal Par, Keogh, B. and Smith, C., Human Kinetics, 1985.

C. Golf Video
Art of Putting, Crenshaw, B., HPG Home Video.
Difficult Shots Made Easy, Irwin, H., Sybervision.
Nancy Lopez—Golf Made Easy, Lopez, N., Media.
Nice Shot, Sports Enhancement Associates.
Women's Golf, Sheehan, P., Sybervision.
Men's Golf, Geiberger, A., Sybervision.

D. Mental Training
Exercise and Mental Health, Morgan, W., and Goldston, S., Hemisphere, 1978.
Mental Game, Loehr, J., Penguin, 1990.
Sports Performance Factors, Rippe, J. and Southmayd, W., Perigee, 1986.

E. Fitness
The Athlete Within, Simon H. and Levisohn, S., Little, Brown and Co., 1987.

E. Humor
Golf Quotes, Great Quotations, 1988.
Sports Quotes, Great Quotations, 1985.
Preferred Lies About Golf: The Real Low Down on the Royal and Ancient Game,
  Dobereimer, P., Harper and Row, 1989.

INDEX

PRE-RECORDED AUDIO TAPES

Some participants in my workshops prefer to have a pre-recorded relaxation/visualization audio tape rather than recite the relaxation text into their own tape recorders. If you prefer this method to making your own tape, please complete the order form below and send it with your check to:

Performance Enhancement Programs (PEP)
5 Longsford
San Antonio, TX 78209

Enclosed is my check for $10.00 (includes postage and handling—Texas residents add sales tax). Please send a pre-recorded tape of the relaxation/visualization exercises contained in Chapters 6-10 to:

_____

_____

_____

PRE-RECORDED AUDIO TAPES

Some participants in my workshops prefer to have a pre-recorded relaxation/visualization audio tape rather than recite the relaxation text into their own tape recorders. If you prefer this method to making your own tape, please complete the order form below and send it with your check to:

Performance Enhancement Programs (PEP)
5 Longsford
San Antonio, TX 78209

Enclosed is my check for $10.00 (includes postage and handling—Texas residents add sales tax). Please send a pre-recorded tape of the relaxation/visualization exercises contained in Chapters 6-10 to:

_____

_____

_____